WRITERS AND T...

ISOBEL AR...
Consulta...

BASIL BUNTING

BASIL
BUNTING

Julian Stannard

NORTHCOTE

BRITISH
COUNCIL

© 2014 by Julian Stannard

First published in 2014 by Northcote House Publishers Ltd, Mary Tavy,
Tavistock, Devon, PL19 9PY, United Kingdom.
Tel: +44 (0) 1822 810066 Fax: +44 (0) 1822 810034.

British Library Cataloguing-in-Publication Data
A catalogue record for this book is available from the British Library

ISBN 978-0-7463-1048-9 hardcover
ISBN 978-0-7463-1006-9 paperback

Typeset by PDQ Typesetting, Newcastle-under-Lyme
Printed and bound in the United Kingdom

In memory of my father

Contents

Acknowledgements

I would like to express my thanks to Bloodaxe for allowing me to cite Bunting's work. Thanks also to colleagues far and wide with whom I have had many invaluable conversations about Bunting. Massimo Bacigalupo sailed me around the Bay of Tigullio so that I could catch sight of Bunting's former home. In particular I would like to thank my colleague Mark Rutter whose readings of *Chomei at Toyama* have been particularly helpful. Also many thanks to Inga Bryden of the University of Winchester who has given a great deal of welcome support to the project.

Biographical Outline

1900	1 March, Basil Cheesman Bunting born in Scotswood-on-Tyne, Northumberland, the son of Thomas Lowe Bunting, a doctor, and Annie Cheesman, who came from a local mining family.
1906	Attends Miss A. M. Bell's kindergarten.
1912–17	Educated at the Quaker schools of Ackworth and Leighton Park.
1913	Possibly first visit to Brigflatts; thereafter several holidays with the Greenbank family. After 1915 some suggestion that Bunting didn't return to Brigflatts until 1965.
1918–19	Arrested as a conscientious objector; he was sentenced to imprisonment at Wormwood Scrubs and Winchester Prison.
1919	Released from Winchester Prison on grounds of ill health.
1920	Enrols at the London School of Economics which he leaves two years later without taking a degree. Secretary to Harry Barnes MP for a brief period.
1920–2	Begins his engagement with London literary life, also becoming an *habitué* of the Fitzroy Tavern in Fitzrovia where he meets the artist Nina Hamnett.
1923–4	Works in Paris, sometimes as a labourer, meets Ezra Pound and subsequently works for Ford Madox Ford on *The Transatlantic Review*.
1924	First visit to Rapallo and during this period starts work on *Villon*.
1925	Death of his father. Bunting returns to England.
1926	Lecturing at Lemington Adult School and in all likelihood living in Throckley.

1927	Works as a music critic for *The Outlook* in London; on the folding of the paper, he enjoys financial support from Margaret de Silver for two years.
1928	Lives and writes in a shepherd's cottage in the Simonside Hills, Northumberland, after which a brief spell in Berlin which gives rise to his poem *Aus Dem Zweiten Reich*.
1929	Returns to Rapallo, and the 'Ezruversity', which is his base until 1933.
1930	First pamphlet collection of poetry, *Redimiculum Matellarum*, is privately published in Milan. Marries Marian Culver in the USA.
1931	First daughter Bourtai born in Genoa. Work is included in Louis Zukofsky's Objectivists issue of *Poetry*, and subsequently in *An 'Objectivists' Anthology*. *Attis* and *Aus Dem Zweiten Reich* written at this time.
1933	The Buntings leave Rapallo for the Canaries. His work is included in Pound's *Active Anthology*.
1934	Second daughter Roudaba born in Santa Cruz de Tenerife.
1935	Writes *The Well of Lycopolis*.
1937	The Buntings separate. Son Rustam born in Wisconsin. On his return to England, Bunting sails his boat the *Thistle* for the best part of a year.
1938	Enrols at Nellist's Nautical School in Newcastle upon Tyne.
1939	Returns from USA on outbreak of Second World War.
1940	Enlists in the RAF, having been rejected by the army and the navy on the grounds of poor eyesight.
1942	Sent to Persia as a translator thanks to his knowledge of classical Persian.
1945–8	By the end of the war has risen to the level of squadron leader, and subsequently works on the British Embassy staff in Tehran.
1948	Marries his second wife, Sima Alladadian. Leaves the embassy and becomes a correspondent for *The Times*.
1950	Daughter of second marriage, Sima-Maria, born. First full-length collection, *Poems 1950*, is published

	by The Cleaners Press, in Texas.
1951	Writes *The Spoils* which is later published in *Poetry* (Chicago).
1951–2	Working again as a correspondent for *The Times* in Tehran from where he is eventually expelled by Mossadeq. Returns with new family and lives with his mother at 242 Newburn Road, Throckley.
1952	Son from second marriage, Thomas Faramaz, is born; first son, Rustam, dies from polio aged 15 in USA.
1954	Takes job as sub-editor on the *Newcastle Daily Journal*, subsequently transferring to the *Newcastle Evening Chronicle* (1957). Deteriorating eyesight: long period of obscurity; Bunting is not writing any poetry.
1963	Begins to be sought out by a younger generation of poets such as Jonathan Williams and Gael Turnbull.
1964	First meeting with Tom Pickard, the youthful catalyst who encourages Bunting to write again, and plays a key part in Bunting's re-discovery through the Morden Tower, which was run by Pickard and his wife Connie.
1965	First major publications in Britain: *The Spoils* (Morden Tower Book Room); *First Book of Odes* and *Loquitur* (both Fulcrum Press). First performance of *Briggflatts* at the Morden Tower, 22 December.
1965	Finishes *Briggflatts*, which he sends to *Poetry* (Chicago).
1966	Publication of *Briggflatts* (Fulcrum Press). Receives Arts Council bursary and retires from the *Evening Chronicle*.
1967	Teaches at the University of California, Santa Barbara. Cataract operations to restore eyesight.
1968	Publication of *Collected Poems* (Fulcrum Press). Appointed to Northern Arts Poetry Fellowship (1968–70) at the Universities of Durham and Newcastle and publication of *Descant on Rawthey's Madrigal*, conversations with Jonathan Williams.
1971	Edits Ford Madox Ford's *Selected Poems*.
1972	President of the Poetry Society.

1974–7	President of Northern Arts.
1976	Edits *Selected Poems* of Joseph Skipsey, Northumberland 'miner' poet.
1978	*Collected Poems* republished by Oxford University Press. Despite newfound poetic status, Bunting's economic situation continues to be fragile and he is forced to move house on several occasions.
1984	Moves to Fox Cottage, Whitley Chapel, near Hexham (Northumberland).
1985	17 April, dies in Hexham General Hospital.

Abbreviations

CP   *Complete Poems* (Newcastle upon Tyne: Bloodaxe, 2000).

D   Jonathan Williams (ed.), *Descant on Rawthey's Madrigal: Conversations with Basil Bunting* (Lexington, Ky.: Gnomon Press, 1968).

M&P   Carroll F. Terrell (ed.), *Basil Bunting: Man and Poet* ed. (Orono, Maine: National Poetry Foundation, 1981).

NB   A Note on *Briggflatts* (1989). This short commentary on *Briggflatts* remains Bunting's only written statement about the poem. It was not readily circulated in his lifetime. The note exists as a single, untitled, typescript in the Basil Bunting Poetry Archive of Durham University Library. It is reproduced in *Basil Bunting: Briggflatts* (Northumberland: Bloodaxe, 2009), 40–1.

PBB   Victoria Forde, *The Poetry of Basil Bunting* (Newcastle upon Tyne: Bloodaxe Books, 1991).

PS   Keith Alldritt, *The Poet as Spy: The Life and Wild Times of Basil Bunting* (London: Arum Press, 1998).

S   A Statement (1966). This can be found at the end of *Descant on Rawthey's Madrigal: Conversations with Basil Bunting* ed. Jonathan Williams or – under the title – 'The Poet's Point of View' (1966) in the *Arts Diary*, Northern Arts (April/Summer, 1966). It is reproduced in *Basil Bunting: Briggflatts* (Northumberland: Bloodaxe, 2009), 42-3.

SV   Peter Makin, *Bunting: The Shaping of His Verse* (Oxford: Clarendon Press, 1992).

1

Introduction

Much of Bunting's standing as a poet rests on the reception of *Briggflatts*. On its publication in 1966 Cyril Connolly described it as 'the finest long poem to be published in England since T. S. Eliot's *Four Quartets*'. The success of *Briggflatts* lifted Bunting out of the obscurity into which he had fallen in the post-war years. It prompted the re-publication of earlier work which allowed readers and critics to evaluate the poet's wider *oeuvre*. For many, *Briggflatts* brought about the 'discovery' of an English poet who had drifted perilously close to becoming an exotic footnote. It is interesting for a moment to compare Bunting's late success with that of the novelist Jean Rhys whose *Wide Sargasso Sea* (1966) brought sudden fame at the age of 76. Both writers had begun their careers in the 1920s, both writers had been part of literary bohemia, both writers had been in different ways associated with Ford Madox Ford, one of the galvanizing forces of modern literature.[1] If *Briggflatts* is the culmination of Bunting's poetic career, the subsequent collection of his work has created a vibrant body of writing spanning some forty years which invites us to re-consider the fault lines that have separated native traditions from more experimental practice. A student of Bunting's work is able to recognize an exemplary dedication to craft and technique which not only reveals a rigorous engagement with modernist poetics but shows how the poet was an intuitive reader of the English tradition. In his post-*Briggflatts* lectures the poet considers, *inter alia*, the significance of Northumbrian art, Wyatt, Spenser and Wordsworth.[2] Bunting was also interested in sung ballads and the oral culture of the north-east.[3] *Complete Poems* (2000), rather in the way of a case study, demonstrates the process by which a master craftsman becomes *sui generis* the master of his art. It includes previously uncollected poems yet maintains a lean muscularity and we know that he wrote a great many poems he later destroyed. Bunting argued that the poet's most important tool was the waste-paper basket.

His resurrection in the 1960s ensures his status in any narrative concerning British modernism. Bunting also made a charismatic contribution to what Eric Mottram called the British Poetry Revival.[4] In fact, the significance of *Briggflatts* gainsays the editors of *The Penguin Book of Contemporary British Poetry* (1982) who promoted their publication on the back of what they perceived as a new spirit in British poetry, emerging after 'a stretch, occupying much of the 1960s and 70s, when very little – in England at any rate – seemed to be happening.'[5] The Morrison/Motion anthology, with its reconfiguration of the centre ground, inevitably distracts us from alternative traditions.[6] Bunting is duly acknowledged in Hugh Kenner's polemic *A Sinking Island* (1988). The Canadian critic, whose *Pound Era* (1971) did much to rehabilitate Ezra Pound after his fall from grace in the 1940s, considers how English writers have all too readily turned their backs on modernist legacies and embraced the spirit of Little England. Bunting is celebrated as a shining exception.[7] Peter Quartermain argues that 'Bunting's position as a writer of English poetry in this century has been notably marginal' which has a deliberateness about it: 'It is part and parcel not only of his identification of himself as a North-umbrian writer, but also of his deliberate and conscious determination to be a *modern* writer.'[8] In fact, Bunting often found himself outside what Auden called 'the tiny jungle' of the literary world.[9]

The story of Bunting is the story of a poet who kept faith with his muse over half a century. Bunting was self-critical and the muse was not always generous. He led an adventurous, sometimes turbulent life and for much of it he was beset by economic difficulties. Bunting, however, was reluctant to compromise and his standards were exacting. Part of the fascination of this narrative comes from observing how Bunting made himself into a poet and how he never reneged on that commitment notwithstanding the complications of his life. Roy Fisher, acknowledging his debt to Bunting, points out that 'he had a variable attitude to his paymasters and benefactors, quite often prickly, particularly when the assistance came from official quarters or from those who would sentimentalize him for he was a very tough man. He kept ready to hand a shifting *persona* [...] I think it gave him some continuity: a device for steering his way through a life that was made up of an unending series of predicaments, some exciting and colourful, some quite desolate.'[10] His success was hard-won and the reader can understand it better by acknowledging an assiduous apprenticeship that has left some exceptional poems along the way. *Briggflatts* is the triumph of forbearance over adversity and its composition drew on a programme of reading, translating and writing that had started in the 1920s. To compose a great poem in your later years is to throw your hat in the ring and come through. Wordsworth, one of Bunting's English influences, acknowledged the power of memory. And Bunting, in what might be seen as a twentieth-century reappraisal of the Romantic formula, wrote 'It is easier to die than to remember' (*CP* 64). His act of remembering has given us one of the great poems of the twentieth century.

2

A Poet's Life

Basil Bunting was born in 1900 in Scotswood-on-Tyne which was then a colliery town on the outskirts of Newcastle. Northumberland, the most northerly part of England, would always be important to Bunting's sense of self.[1] In effect, the poet came from a geographical location with a distinct regional and cultural identity which set him apart from those writers who more readily identified with the capital's metropolitan culture. Quartermain acknowledges the influence of the Newcastle Literary and Philosophical Society on the poet's early education. Bunting read Cuthbert Sharp's *The Rising of the North* which documented the Catholic uprising of 1569. Queen Elizabeth's response was swift and brutal. Following the orders of the Earl of Sussex, Sir George Bowes 'marched [...] through Tynedale and Redesdale killing plundering and destroying, saying "the best fruit a tree can beare is a dead traytour"'.[2] As a young man in his twenties, now sometimes living in London, Bunting encountered the modishness of metropolitan Bloomsbury with a marked lack of enthusiasm. His attachment to Northumberland might also be contrasted with Philip Larkin's provincial niggardliness.

Larkin's attitude is demonstrated in 'I Remember, I Remember', a poem whose withering metaphysic leans ironically on Thomas Hood's nineteenth-century evocation of halcyon childhood.[3] Larkin's poem is about Coventry, the place of his birth, a city later destroyed by the Luftwaffe. The poem takes the form of a train conversation in which the poet-speaker remains resolutely disenchanted. The train comes to a stop and the speaker looks out and exclaims: 'Why Coventry! [...] I was born here'. This provides an opportunity for a catalogue of *non events* and the fellow passenger asks whether he 'wished the place in

Hell'. The speaker claims, in that existentially unnerving final line, that 'Nothing, like anything, happens anywhere'. Larkin had a talent for fuelling the anodyne with a special turbo charge. The train was in all likelihood on the way to Hull where Larkin lived most of his adult life. Here he affected a calculated retreat into provincial suburbia where he cultivated the poetic ideology that had many of its premises in his 1955 'Statement'. The inaccessibility of Hull suited Larkin too. He liked to think of all those Americans 'getting on to the train at King's Cross and thinking they're going to come and bother me, and then looking at the connections and deciding they'll go to Newcastle and bother Basil Bunting instead.'[4]

Northumberland for Bunting was always a place of geographical and historical significance. Keeping faith with William Carlos Williams' argument that 'the true universal is the local', Bunting's commitment to the north never precluded an enthusiasm for wider international perspectives.[5] This outward-looking regionalism suggests common purpose with the London-Welsh poet David Jones and the Marxist Scottish poet Hugh MacDiarmid as well as English poets such as Charles Tomlinson and Roy Fisher, all of whom remained sympathetic to the modernist project yet were similarly wedded to British location.[6] This relationship between the local and the international is of particular importance in *Briggflatts*.

Bunting's biography – literary and otherwise – is fraught with twists and turns. Victoria Forde points out that Bunting's life is spiced with 'the material of novels' (*PBB* 46); Peter Makin talks of a poet of 'legends' (*SV* 93). Carroll F. Terrell entitles his biographical account of the poet 'An Eccentric Profile' (*M&P* 25–6) and Keith Alldritt's biography enjoys the rambunctious title *The Poet as Spy: The Life and Wild Times of Basil Bunting*. We need to add to these W. B. Yeats' description of the English poet as 'one of Ezra's more savage disciples' and we begin to see how Bunting's life seems to take on the drama of an Elizabethan courtier, rather in the manner of Walter Raleigh (*SV* 24). Larkin, leading light of the post-war *derrière-garde*, celebrated the commonplace. In contrast, the trajectory of Bunting's career takes on a quasi-Byronic quality. The German critic Peter Burger argues in *Theory of the Avant-Garde* that modernism is less a break with the nineteenth century than 'the last gasp of romanticism'[7]

5

and although biographical readings of Bunting's work under-estimate the wider strategies of his poetry, it is easy to see why commentators might dwell on the extraordinary circumstances of the *poète maudit*. Towards the end of the fourth section of *Briggflatts* we are presented with the poet as habitual outsider: 'Where rats go go I,/accustomed to penury,/filth, disgust and fury' (CP 77).

The biography is one of vicissitudes even though Bunting was born into a solidly middle-class household. His mother was the daughter of a local mining engineer and his father was a doctor who was interested in the histology of mammalian lymphatic glands. We are given accounts of a household which was sometimes overrun by lizards and it is interesting to consider how the father's science informed the son's poetry. Lizards notwithstanding, Bunting was brought up 'in an atmosphere of music, poetry and Quakerism'. He boarded at the Quaker schools of Ackworth in Yorkshire and then later at Leighton Park in Berkshire. In keeping with Nonconformist practice, Bunting's religious education ensured a familiarity with the Bible, not least the Song of Songs and the Books of Kings. If at Leighton Park we discover the youthful poet giving a paper on Kerensky, Russia's provisional prime minister in 1917, we learn at Ackworth how the 15-year-old had discovered Walt Whitman's *Leaves of Grass*. The discovery is both significant and emblematic. Whitman's Amer-ican poetic provides a bracing alternative to the etiolated romanticism of the prevailing Georgian attitude as well as a foretaste of Bunting's later engagement with American poetry. Quartermain considers the way in which Bunting follows Pound and Whitman in his attention to the sonic and musical possibilities of poetry (M&P 145–58). The schoolboy wrote an essay on Whitman which won a national prize and which drew him to the attention of 'an old gentleman living in Sheffield who got on his pushbike and rode thirty or forty miles in order to call on the 15-year-old critic of Whitman' (M&P 30). The man in question was Edward Carpenter, friend of Whitman, Fabian and social activist. This youthful encounter with Carpenter antici-pated the great number of important literary figures who would touch upon the poet's life.[8]

As a conscientious objector from the Quaker tradition, Bunting refused to enlist on his eighteenth birthday. He also refused to do agricultural work in order to release men for the front and although the First World War was over by November 1918 he found himself in Wormwood Scrubs sentenced to hard labour. By 1919 Bunting was in Winchester Prison where he went on hunger strike and the prison governor attempted to break him by having a freshly roasted chicken sent to his cell each day. The tactic failed to work and the 'chicken incident' eventually found its way into Ezra Pound's *Cantos*.[9] Bunting's prison experiences led to his contribution to Graham Wallas' book on the harshness of prison conditions that was later put before the Royal Commission. After he'd dropped out of the London School of Economics and had worked briefly for Harry Barnes, Liberal MP for East Newcastle, he moved to Paris. Here he met Ezra Pound and become a youthful member of the émigré community. He worked variously as a road builder, a barman and as the amanuensis and general factotum of Ford Madox Ford who was setting up *The Transatlantic Review*. Bunting in his twenties was not averse to drinking and occasional brawling and his next major brush with the law came in 1923.

Bunting records an evening of heavy drinking in Paris which ended up in a drunken attempt to get back into a hotel that wasn't in fact the hotel he had booked into. Whilst the husband of the concierge sought the police the concierge herself invited him into her room. Although Bunting tells us she was fairly old she apparently made up for it by 'a whole lot of enthusiasm' (*M&P* 42). The arrival of the police led to further fracas and Bunting was charged with not only disturbing the peace but with resisting arrest and the more serious count of 'rebellion'. The following day Bunting was taken to the *grande salle* of the Santé Prison and the narration now switches from quasi-fabliau to one that is charged with an uncanny historical resonance. The poet found himself amongst 'a flock of petty thieves, pickpockets, prostitutes, pimps' (*M&P* 42). Bunting, quite appropriately, had a copy of Villon in his pocket which he began to read, not unaware of the irony. The French poet had sat in the same room waiting to be sentenced some four hundred years beforehand. Having received notice from Bunting, Pound arrived at the prison duly impressed to find the Englishman reading Villon *in situ*.

To be reading François Villon in the Santé Prison whilst awaiting the magistrate was in itself an act of subversion. Villon's bid for survival in the brutalizing milieu of fifteenth-century Paris made him the poet of transgression *par excellence* whose sardonic insights spoke to the twentieth century. Pound's interest in Villon had been manifested in *The Spirit of Romance* (1910). For Pound, the Frenchman was 'a lurid canto of the Inferno, written too late to be included in the original text' (*PS* 35). By 1923 Pound was working on his opera *Le Testament de Villon*. Not only quarrying modernist tropes of displacement and cultural opposition, he was prefiguring his own later incarceration which was punishment for the infamous Roman Broadcasts made during the 1940s. Villon, in effect, became part of the modernist lexicon. Holed up in St Elizabeth's Hospital in the 1950s, Pound declared 'I seem to be born to be jailed'.[10] Pound had passed his enthusiasm for Villon onto Bunting whose own experiences of prison enlivened the French poet beyond academic interest. This act of identification is converted into *Villon*, Bunting's first major poem.

THE RAPALLO YEARS

Hugh Selwyn Mauberley (1920) with its excoriating reappraisal of post-1918 imperial Britain for whom so many had recently died – 'an old bitch gone in the teeth/[...] a botched civilization' – was Pound's literary valediction to London. By 1924 Paris had also lost its allure and the Pounds had identified the Ligurian town of Rapallo, down the coast from Genoa, as an ideal place to set up home. Pound had given Bunting his Italian address and the Englishman now back in Newcastle decided to renew his association with the American poet. The journey to Rapallo wasn't without incident. Bunting was arrested for a drinking episode and a letter was sent to Ford explaining that he was now in a Genoese jail, which resulted in a letter from Ernest Hemingway to Pound suggesting that the Italian authorities might be approached on Bunting's behalf. Having extricated himself from this temporary incarceration, the young English poet reached Rapallo to find the Pounds were out of town. Yet the beauty of the place was not lost on him and Bunting stayed put exploring the Ligurian landscape. From Bunting's conversation with Jonathan Williams we learn further details. The English poet had decided to climb a mule track which arrived at an inn at the top of a mountain. As he passed the *locale* someone started shouting his name and to his surprise he discovered Ezra Pound calling after him. The account continues: 'Ezra was very pleasant and it was from that meeting that I can say that I became one of Pound's friends [and] I never lost touch with him again' (*D*). It was a friendship that was later strained by ideological differences but in these early formative years there is little doubt that the Poundian impact was integral to his development as a poet. This first sojourn in Rapallo not only paved the way for a later and longer attachment to the place but also showed how this very English poet was ever receptive to wider cultural influences.

This period in Rapallo lasted about a year. Bunting found work on the sand boats which shuttled down to Tuscany and across to Sardinia. Pound had observed how the head-sacks worn by the sand carriers looked like the Phrygian beret of Odysseus.[11] Bunting's early experience of seafaring anticipated later episodes, including his enrolment at the Nellist Nautical Academy in Newcastle in the 1930s. It also inculcated something of the spirit of the 'Odyssean' poet – resourceful, open to experience and alert to the age-old culture of the Mediterranean. Mottram observes how Bunting 'frequently presents tides, pools, harbours, open sea, whirlpools, waterfalls and streams as instances of clarity and pollution, freedom and stagnation, mobility and clogged fixity, fertility and sterility' (*M&P* 94). Bunting met up with Pound on a regular basis for several months and it was in this period, not without the help of Pound's editorial blue pencil, that he worked on *Villon*. Bunting argued that 'Pound must have chopped out at least one fifth, perhaps one quarter of the last two parts [...] He didn't touch the third part.'[12] News of his father's ill health obliged Bunting to cut short this first Rapallesian visit and he was forced to try out his luck in England. Back in Newcastle in 1926 Bunting had first hand experience of the miners' strike which later spread to the General Strike. Bunting's father had always been sympathetic to the miners' plight and the son was active in supporting their cause and forcefully resisting the government strategy of strike-breaking which meant inevitable run-ins with the police themselves.[13]

The apprentice poet later found himself gravitating towards London to look for work. After he had been released from Winchester Prison in 1919 Bunting had become familiar with the capital, sometimes eating without expense at the Common Room of the Fabian Society and soon becoming an *habitué* of the Fitzroy Tavern in Fitzrovia. It had been set up by the Russian émigré Papa Judah Kleinfeldt, formerly a soldier in the czarist army. Earning a legendary status in the London of the 1920s, the pub functioned as a literary salon with plentiful amounts of alcohol. Here Bunting met the artist Nina Hamnett who helped engineer the poet's entry into the bohemian worlds of London and Paris. Kleinfeldt and the heady culture of the Fitzroy Tavern would be remembered in the second section of *Briggflatts*. It was in this first London phase that Bunting came across Pound's *Homage to Sextus Propertius* and Eliot's 'Preludes', both of which awakened him to the musical possibilities of poetry.

Back in London after his return from Rapallo, Bunting's financial position was less than secure. A little serendipity eased the situation. The American literary editor Otto Theiss offered him the job as a music critic for *The Outlook*. Until the closure of the newspaper in 1928 Bunting drew on his musical interests, which had been generated by listening to the Newcastle Bach Choir in Durham Cathedral as a boy, to hone his journalistic skills and develop his theories about poetry and music. The job was paid enough to allow a reasonable living and his pieces were successful enough to encourage the editors of the *Musical Times* and *The Times* to commission work from him. The relationship with *The Times*, though inconsistent, would last a couple of decades and, in another context, it would be interesting to dwell on the relationship between Bunting the poet and Bunting the journalist. Donald Wesling, referring to correspondence between Bunting and Peter Makin, draws attention to the 'hell section' of *Briggflatts* and we now know that 'Hastor' – 'One/plucked fruit warm from the arse/[...] Hastor! Hastor!' (*CP* 71) – is a reference to Hugh Astor of *The Times*. Although Bunting, at different moments of his life, would operate both outside and within the establishment, Wesling acknowledges the poet's 'rejection of the social dirt language of journalism' and sees his habitual strategy as 'resisting and modifying [...] official discourse'.[14] After the folding of *The Outlook*, Bunting had the fortune to discover a patron in the guise of Margaret de Silver. An American widow, whose husband had been one of the founders of the Civil Liberties Union, de Silver had inherited considerable wealth which she spent on 'subsidising artists, poets, politicians, lawyers, civil liberties' (*D*). Having met Bunting in London she was impressed by his dedication to poetry and granted him the sum of £200 for two years, though her generosity extended intermittently beyond that period. This allowed him in the first instance to take on a shepherd's cottage in the Simonside Hills in Northumberland where he learnt about the training of sheep dogs, an experience which makes its way into the final section of *Briggflatts*. Thereafter, he spent a short joyless period in Berlin prompting *Aus Dem Zweiten Reich*, after which he returned to Rapallo which remained his base until 1933.

Bunting's personal circumstances had changed on meeting Margaret Culver in Venice in 1929. They were married on Long Island in 1930 and Bunting unsuccessfully sought work in a country that was reeling from the Wall Street Crash of 1929. Bunting's economic difficulties on both sides of the Atlantic and his consciousness of political crisis inform much of his early work. However, the American visit did allow Bunting to renew his relationship with the poet Louis Zukofsky whom he had first met in Rapallo. Bunting also became acquainted with René Taupin and William Carlos Williams. Margaret de Silver's financial assistance having now ended, the Buntings returned to Rapallo which allowed the English poet to re-enrol at what came to be known as the 'Ezruversity'.

The Ligurian coast – the Italian Riviera – had long attracted foreign writers and Rapallo became the place of choice. Bunting, in effect, was re-joining an émigré community of writers, artists and musicians (which included Pound's mistress Olga Rudge) who were able to set up home in an idyllic location without enormous expense. For a while Bunting took on a cottage near the village of San Bartolomeo. If Pound was the head professor at the 'Ezruversity', the faculty and its students were equally impressive. Earlier visitors had included Hemingway and Eliot, and by 1929 Yeats was spending considerable periods on the

Italian Riviera. Pound had come to London in 1909 to sit at the feet of the Irish poet and became a regular at Yeats' literary 'Mondays' at the Woburn Buildings. Yeats' association with Rapallo would last four years and references are made to the Ligurian town in the Irish poet's prose piece *A Packet for Ezra Pound* (1929). Pound documents Yeats' response to Rapallo: '"Sligo in heaven" murmured uncle William/when the mist finally settled down on Tigullio' (*Cantos* LXXVII). The Irishman was joining the 'Rapallo Group' as an internationally acclaimed poet.[15] At first he was wary of Bunting, comparing him with that rather dangerous coterie of young men which surrounded Shakespeare's theatre 'when it was denounced by the first puritans'.[16] Yet the relationship became warmer and the English poet was surprised at a dinner hosted by Yeats in which the Nobel Prize winner recited one of Bunting's poems from memory.[17]

Bunting's second period in Rapallo was fruitful. *Villon*, which had been written during his earlier stay, was published in *Poetry* in 1930. The Chicago-based magazine established by Harriet Monroe played an important role in promoting the values of modernist poetry and remained sympathetic to Bunting's poetry over the years.[18] In 1930 Bunting's first volume *Redimiculum Matellarum* (Necklace of Chamber Pots) was published privately in Milan. By 1931 he had written both *Attis: Or, Something Missing* and *Aus Dem Zweiten Reich*. Zukofsky's Objectivist issue of *Poetry* containing Bunting's 'The Word' ('Nothing') also came out in 1931. In October 1933, by which time the Buntings had decamped to Tenerife, Faber and Faber brought out Pound's *Active Anthology* which was dedicated to Bunting and Zukofsky and which contained a substantial amount of the Englishman's work. Bunting was working on shorter poems too and his musical interests were also kept alive. Together with Ezra Pound and Eugen Haas, the English poet was helping to organize concerts at the town hall of Rapallo.[19] And he had the opportunity to carry out further journalistic work. In 1932 Pound persuaded the local newspaper *Il Mare* to incorporate a literary supplement which became for a short period (1932–3) an ambitious cosmopolitan vehicle for the writers and artists of Rapallo. Bunting's name appears on the masthead of the *Supplemento Letterario*, along with Pound and

Francesco Monotti, under *Affari Esteri* (Foreign Literature). One finds references to Constantin Brancusi, Gaudier-Brzeska, William Carlos Williams, Jules Laforgue, W. B. Yeats and many others among its pages. The improbability of this small Riviera town hosting such an international publication provides one of the fascinating footnotes of the period.[20]

In Rapallo Bunting continued to submit himself to the Poundian discipline of 'translation'. Reading foreign poetry introduced an apprentice poet to varying cadences which the American considered essential to a poet's development. Poetic translation and adaptation were integral to modernist practice *per se*. Pound's *Homage to Sextus Propertius* and the *Cathay* poems had provided palpable examples; Bunting's engagement with Villon demonstrated that he was working along similar lines. He was also working from the Latin poets Lucretius, Horace and Catullus as well as translating and adapting his 'Japanese' poem *Chomei at Toyama* (1932), sections of which appeared in *Poetry* in 1933. Bunting made use of an Italian translation of the *Hō-Jō-Ki*, originally written by Kamo-no-Chomei in 1212. The Italian text had been a chance find on the quayside of Genoa; I like to imagine it was in Piazza Banchi where a second-hand book business is still in evidence. A later discovery in the port area of the city would have a significance that Bunting could hardly have imagined. He came across a tattered and incomplete nineteenth-century French translation of the *Shahnameh* by the tenth-century Persian poet Firdosi. Bunting read the epical 'Book of Kings' to the Pounds who were equally fascinated but the translation only took them halfway through the text. Pound, therefore, bought Bunting the complete three-volume text in Persian and Bunting set himself the task of learning classical Persian in order to translate it into English. The exercise provided him with a linguistic skill that would change the course of his life.

BUNTING OF PERSIA 1942–52

When Britain declared war with Germany in 1939 Bunting was in the United States. William Carlos Williams writes in his *Autobiography*: 'Bunting has been a conscientious objector in the

13

First World War and they had given him some rough treatment. It is worth noting, however, that for the Second World War he rushed across the United States from California to go to England, as fast as he could, to enlist.'[21] Bunting's enthusiasm for the war against Nazi-Fascism reflected his left-leaning sympathies. His years in Italy and the later joyless period in Tenerife on the eve of the Spanish Civil War (1933–6) meant that the rising power of the right had been experienced close at hand. One of Bunting's occasional adversaries at the chess board was the military governor of the Canary Islands, Francisco Franco. In 1936 he wrote an essay for *The Spectator* entitled 'The Roots of the Spanish Civil War'. Bunting, now in America, was appalled to see a letter that his friend Zukofsky had received from Pound full of 'anti-semite bile' (*PS* 94). Bunting wrote back to signal his disgust with Pound's politics. Although their friendship would survive, Bunting distanced himself from the American's 'maniacally fascist' views.[22]

The Second World War offered the possibility of assuming a more heroic role after the travails, economic and domestic, that befell Bunting in the 1930s. *The Well of Lycopolis* (1935), as we shall later see, is a particularly anguished, misanthropic piece. By 1937 his wife had left him, taking their two young daughters back to Wisconsin. She was pregnant with the son Bunting would never get a chance to see. He dealt with this separation by buying the *Thistle* which he sailed alone around Essex and the coast of Devon helping out with the local fishermen. The beginning of the war for Bunting, however, was less than glamorous. At the age of 40 he was having some difficulty in finding a useful role, managing at last to get into the RAF, notwithstanding his poor eyesight (*PS* 97). Aircraftsman Bunting worked with reconnaissance and anti-aircraft balloons. For a while he was stationed in Hull, where he only just escaped a bombing raid, and then he found himself in Scotland working aboard a converted luxury yacht called the *Golden Hind*. The breakthrough came when Bunting wrote to the Air Ministry drawing their attention to his knowledge of Persian. In 1942 he was posted to Persia as an interpreter.

There was a difference between the classical Persian he had taught himself in order to translate the *Shahnameh* and the modern Farsi spoken in Tehran. Bunting explains that before arriving in the country he'd never heard the language spoken and that soon after his arrival he had to interpret at a court martial: 'You can imagine how difficult that was', he says, 'I hope they put the right man in jail. Very fortunately it wasn't one of those cases where it would require shooting or hanging' (D). Yet his grasp of classical Persian proved no handicap when it came to dealing with the Bakhtiari tribesmen whose dialect is not unlike medieval Persian (D). An official interpreter for a RAF squadron based in the Bakhtiari region, Bunting was assigned to work with these fiercely independent nomadic peoples and the posting proved a success. He would later tell Zukofsky that he loved them 'as burningly as ever I loved' (PS 103), and he described their unstinting hospitality which included 'pipes and drums, dancers and singers, sweetmeats and rice and strong drink and a man to fan [him] all the evening' (PBB 47). In the First World War, T. E. Lawrence had worked alongside and commanded Arabs in their revolt against Ottoman rule and the story was later mythologized in David Lean's *Lawrence of Arabia* (1962). Bunting's Persian exploits are rather less documented and the Official Secrets Act has deterred further investigation. Yet the strategic importance of the Persian oil supplies meant that until their defeat at Stalingrad the Germans had designs on the area. The aim of German intelligence was to win support for the Axis cause and in particular they set out to gain influence among the Bakhtiari whose lands bordered Iraq which had seen in Rashid Ali a pro-Nazi prime minister. Bunting became involved in the struggle between the pro-German and the pro-British clans within the Bakhtiari and after the war he claimed that 'He had quelled a German-aided revolt of the Bakhtiari tribesmen almost single-handed, and to that extent he may have altered the course of the war, for the Germans were within an ace of succeeding in creating a foothold in Persia' (PS 103).

After Montgomery's success at El Alamein in 1942 and the pivotal battle of Stalingrad in 1943, the balance of the war was changing. It was decided that the weaponry and ammunition stockpiled in Persia for defensive purposes would now be more useful to the Eighth Army. Bunting was involved in both organizing and driving these supplies to Tripoli. Alldritt describes the journey in *The Poet as Spy*. The point of departure was Basra in the Persian Gulf and the route, some 1,500 miles, took them across the deserts of southern Iraq and Saudi Arabia, over the Red Sea and on through Egypt into Libya. The journey took a month. When the convoy passed the battlefields near to Tripoli, Bunting could see that the desert was littered with the detritus of war – broken tanks, aeroplane fuselages, abandoned cars, German trucks still with their rations of beer, enemy prisoners marching eastwards (*PS* 104). The experience made its way into his poem *The Spoils* (1951). As the Eighth Army was preparing for the invasion of Sicily, Bunting was promoted to the rank of pilot officer. He now found himself in Italy again where his knowledge of both the Italian language and Italian geography made him useful to the war effort. In July 1943, he helped arrange General Eisenhower's war-room (*PS* 106) and also helped co-ordinate the allied landings, playing no small part in the capture of the Calabrian town of Crotone. Intriguingly, as he later explained to Dorothy Pound, one of his tasks was to brief the American pilots who were instructed to bomb the Zoagli viaduct in Liguria (*PS* 106). Poor weather conditions meant that bombs were actually released on Rapallo. The Pounds by this time had been asked by the authorities to leave their house in Via Marsala and they were taken in by Pound's mistress Olga Rudge, who lived up in Sant'Ambrogio. Pound refers to this local bombardment in his writing, yet for him there was worse to come. After having made his Roman Broadcasts he was already a *persona non grata* and had been indicted *in absentia* in July 1943. When the war was over he was arrested by partisans and handed over to the American authorities, resulting in his internment at Metato near Pisa. Bunting and his former mentor had found themselves on opposing sides and there appears to be an ironic symbolism in the bombing of Rapallo.

Bunting had a good war. In 1945 he wrote to Zukofsky:

> [M]y taste for variety has certainly been gratified in this war. I have been on almost every British front worth being on except Dunkirk, travelled through every rank from aircraftsman First Class to Squadron-Leader (equals Major, to forestall your question), seen huge chunks of the world that I wouldn't otherwise have visited, been sailor, balloon-man, drill instructor, interpreter, truck driver in the desert, intelligence officer to a busy fighter squadron, recorder of

16

the doings of nomadic tribes, labour manager, and now consul in a more or less crucial post. (*M&P* 57)

The ending of the war had offered no obvious outlet to Bunting apart from frugal living and further writing but the Foreign Office, thanks to the prompting of MI6, offered him the position of British vice consul at Isfahan (*PS* 107). In June 1946, when the post came to an end, Bunting returned to his mother's house in Northumberland. The contrast between Isfahan and the strictures of post-war England can only be imagined. Dorothy Pound was planning to send over food parcels yet this proved unnecessary as Bunting was offered a new role at the embassy in Tehran as chief of political intelligence, a post he took up in 1947. In a life of changing fortunes, which had included homelessness and stints in prison, this period constitutes one of the high points of the poet's life. He was given a comfortable house, enjoyed working with the ambassador Sir John Le Rougetel and became friends with Ronald Oakshot, another intelligence officer whom he described as a 'hard-drinking ex-British officer, "gone native"' (*PS* 113). Oakshot was married to an Iranian woman whose younger sister was to become Bunting's second wife. Sima Alladallian, half Armenian, half Kurd, was the younger daughter of a wealthy pro-British Iranian family whose father had worked for the Anglo-Iranian Oil Company. Only 14 when she married Bunting, the marriage legitimate under Iranian law, she would go with Bunting back to Northumberland after his later expulsion from Iran. The marriage meant, however, that he had to relinquish his position at the embassy. After honeymooning in England with his new bride, he returned to Tehran as a correspondent for *The Times* which provided adequate cover for his intelligence work. Bunting continued to read and translate Persian poetry. In 1953, he is writing to Zukofsky: 'It is no boast to say that I am more widely read in Persian than most of the Orientalists in the British and European universities, especially in early poets – Firdosi, Rudaki, Manuchehri, Farrukhi, etc, whose work is fundamental to a real understanding of Persian literature in the same way that the work of Homer and Aeschylus is funda-mental to an understanding of the Greek' (*PBB* 121). This engagement with Persian culture would influence his later work.

By April 1950 Bunting was back in Throckley, Northumberland. By October of that year the poet and his young family had moved to Lido di Camaiore, near Lucca in Tuscany. Journalism once again provided Bunting with a cover for his intelligence work as he took on a role as foreign correspondent for the *Northern Echo*. In the war's aftermath the political situation in Italy was of concern to America and Britain who feared that strong communist sympathies within the country might steer Italy towards the Soviet Union. Alldritt intimates that this was a particularly dangerous period for Bunting, necessitating a swift retreat from the country (*PS* 132). By 1951 he found himself back in Persia working for *The Times* but this proved to be his last visit. Mossadeq, who nationalized the Anglo-Iranian Oil Company on becoming prime minister, created a climate of high tension especially for foreign personnel, many of whom quickly left. This didn't, however, prevent Bunting from resuming a comfortable lifestyle. We get a description of Bunting's Persian idyll in Robert Payne's *Journey to Persia* (1951):

> I spent the days bathing in this waterfall in the garden of an English poet not far from Shamran, up the sloping role which eventually loses itself in the snows of the Elbruz mountains. It was a small garden, full of dying roses, for summer was coming on. There was a red-tiled swimming pool, and the poet was credited with possessing the best cook and the best collection of whisky in Teheran. He possessed a passionate love of Persia, translated their poetry superbly, knew many Persian dialects and thought the world and ambition well lost as long as he could remain in the garden, with his exquisitely handsome Armenian wife, his books and his pipes. He had been in the British Secret Service, held – and this was one of the most astonishing things about him – the rank of Squadron-Leader in The R.A.F, and was known in Teheran for the wisdom of his political judgements. He had known everyone, and was afraid of no one. He looked like an intelligent monkey, and there was something in the quick sharp voice which reminded you of Socrates. (*M&P* 58)

The situation was, however, potentially dangerous. Bunting talks of how 'two men with pistols arrived at our door while I was taking an afternoon nap. My wife told them I wasn't in [...] and [they] went away again' (*D*). The quasi-comical dimension of these incidents is summed up in the story about the Ritz Hotel. Bunting, who was in the flat of a Reuters correspondent, heard a hired mob baying for his life outside the hotel: 'I said what the hell, no one knows what I look like or anything. I went out. I walked into the crowd and stood amongst them and shouted DEATH TO MR BUNTING! with the best of them and nobody took the slightest notice of me' (*D*). In April 1952, Mossadeq, unimpressed by Bunting's candid reporting and no doubt conscious of his undercover activities, expelled the former diplomat. Bunting loaded up a dilapidated Ford Mercury and drove his family to Baghdad. From there they drove to Damascus and then on to Istanbul, and travelling across Europe, they finally made their way to Northumberland.

RETURN TO THE NORTH 1952–85

The return to England was a return to a bleak post-war reality. The country was bankrupt and rationing was in force until 1954. Having lived in exotic, far-flung places, Bunting found himself at his mother's house in a colliery town, unemployed and with a young family in tow. His experiences with the Foreign Office and *The Times* cut little ice. Terrell argues that because Bunting had no university qualifications and because 'he was muzzled by the Official Secrets Act from detailing his experiences, he was unable to get work in which his amazing creative talents could be used' (*M&P* 60). Bunting learnt that the Iranian authorities had sequestered his possessions in Tehran, including his library of Persian texts which had taken twenty years to build up (PS 141). Worse news came when he learnt that Rustam, his 15-year-old son whom he had never seen, had died from polio in America. The grief of this is expressed in 'A Song for Rustam' (*CP* 197) which Bunting never allowed to be published in his lifetime. After periods of freelancing and proof-reading he finally gained employment working night shifts as a sub-editor for the *Newcastle Daily Journal* and later he took up employment with the *Newcastle Evening Chronicle*. Stultifying provincial journalism became the mainstay of his working life.

This fall in fortune was matched by a hiatus on the literary front. After the publication of *The Spoils* in 1951 thirteen long years would pass before Bunting's literary career got back on track. There had been some limited success in America when

Dallam Flynn, an admirer of Pound, published *Poems 1950*. In his introduction Flynn beats a loud drum for the English poet arguing that the publication was a way of fighting the '*suppressing* for nearly two decades' of 'Bunting's magnificent verse' (*PBB* 51). Peter Russell, who had published Bunting in the magazine *Nine*, was unwilling to publish a British edition of *Poems 1950* and Eliot turned against the project finding the work unduly influenced by Pound (*PS* 133). Undoubtedly, Bunting's trying personal circumstances mitigated against creativity. Yet these long years of poetic drought also coincided with a cultural landscape which was unsympathetic to Bunting's style of poetry. In 1955 Larkin published his 'Statement': 'As a guiding principle, I believe that every poem must be its own sole freshly created universe, and therefore have no belief in "tradition" or a common myth-kitty or casual allusions in poems to other poems or poets.'[23] Eliot's essay 'Tradition and Individual Talent' is clearly within his sights here and Larkin and the group of writers which became known as the Movement could be seen as resisting not only the bardic excesses of Dylan Thomas and the Neo-Apocalyptic poets of the 1940s but also the international programme that lay at the heart of modernist poetry. The title of Larkin's first significant collection – *The Less Deceived* (1955) – heralds a new kind of English pragmatism and the poet-critic Donald Davie has described this post-war retrenchment as 'a lowering of horizons and a pulling in of horns' as if out of the brouhaha of modernist experiment there was in keeping with the austerity of post-war Britain an appetite for modesty and restraint. Kingsley Amis called for no more poems 'about philosophers or paintings or novelists or art galleries or mythology or foreign cities or other poems'.[24] The Movement set itself against a poetry of experiment and allusiveness in its attempt to restore the 'English' line. As bombed English cities were in the process of being rebuilt, the Movement sought to reconstruct traditional prosodic virtues after what many had seen as the rupturing influences of an imported modernist poetic. When the Movement anthology *New Lines* was published in 1956, Robert Conquest used an orchestral metaphor to argue that the mistake had been made 'of giving the Id, a sound player on the percussion side under a strict conductor, too much of a say in the doings of the orchestra as a whole'.[25] Romantic-modernist swagger gave way to small-gestured ironies and narrow empiricism. By the late 1950s Bunting would have seemed rather like a paid-off soldier from an earlier campaign. The ageing poet, who had at times been at the hub of the modernist project, was sinking into obscurity.

Bunting's later Northumbrian period can be divided into the wilderness years prior to the publication of *Briggflatts* and the resurrection that came in its wake. How it came about has its own quasi-mythological dimension. The catalyst came in the form of the 17-year-old Tom Pickard who edited a magazine called *Eruption* and had hopes of becoming a poet himself. Interested in American poetry, as an antidote to the prevailing Movement manner, Pickard had contacted Jonathan Williams in North Carolina who gave him Bunting's address. In 1963 the working-class boy of left-wing persuasions arrived at the home of the former squadron leader, drank whisky and listened to Bunting reading *The Spoils*.[26] The evening was the start of a long-lasting friendship that pushed Bunting back into writing. Pickard and his partner Connie had set up a bookshop and reading room at the Morden Tower, a medieval building in a less than salubrious area bordering on 'Shaggers' Alley' (*PS* 149). Bunting was soon reading at the gas-lit Tower to a newfound audience, 'the unabashed boys and girls' who became the youthful constituent of the British Poetry Revival of the 1960s and 1970s. In a period of student unrest, Bunting 'seemed somehow to represent both tradition and rebellion'.[27] Pickard had *The Spoils* re-published by the Morden Tower Book Room and in 1964 Bunting was telling Zukofsky: 'Somehow the old machine has been set to work again and I have actually been writing' (*PBB* 58). 1965 becomes Bunting's *annus mirabilis*. The Fulcrum Press published the *First Book of Odes*, followed by *Loquitur* and in 1966 they brought out *Briggflatts*. The success of his long poem and the re-publication of earlier works not only brought Bunting late recognition, it changed the course of his life. Honours, awards and titles now came his way. Leaving the *Evening Chronicle* in 1966, he flew off to America to take up a visiting lectureship at the University of California. There would be more teaching posts as well as tours in America and Canada and in 1968 Bunting was appointed Northern Arts Literary Fellow at Newcastle and Durham Universities and in that same year Fulcrum published his *Collected Poems*. In 1972 he was appointed President of the Poetry Society and in 1974 he became President of Northern Arts. Biographical and literary interest, sometimes in the form of film and documentaries, continued apace until the end of his life. Perhaps the most memorable of these is Peter Bell's film *Basil Bunting: An Introduction to the Work of a Poet* (1982). Made three years before Bunting died, the film shows an aged, charismatic poet surrounded by the landscape and iconography of his landmark poem: Throckley bull, Northumbrian sheep, the stone-mason at work in the graveyard and the all-important Quaker meeting house.

3

The Early Sonatas: *Villon, Attis: Or, Something Missing, The Well of Lycopolis, Aus Dem Zweiten Reich*

In his preface to the *Collected Poems* (1968) Bunting acknowledges his debts to 'poets long dead'. The list included Dante, Wordsworth, Whitman, Wyatt, Malherbe, Spenser and Firdosi. Writing to Zukofsky in the early 1950s, Bunting also refers to the influence of Lucretius and Horace as well as classicial Persian poetry (*PBB* 250). In the preface he adds: 'but two living men also taught me much: Ezra Pound and in his sterner, stonier way, Louis Zukofsky. It would not be fitting to collect my poems without mentioning them.' Bunting's association with Pound and Zukofsky would, at first sight, position the English poet firmly within a well-documented modernist tradition and the significance of his apprenticeship at the Ligurian 'Ezruversity' has been noted. Bunting's work appeared in the special Objectivist issue of *Poetry* 1931, whose theory was formulated in Zukofsky's essay 'Program: "Objectivists" 1931'. Paying particular reference to the poetry of Charles Reznikoff, Zukofsky describes a process of 'objectification' in which the poem, now working against Romantic notions of self-expression, takes on the form of an object, solid and complete in itself. Although Bunting objected to Zukofsky's theoretical programme by publishing an open letter in the *Supplemento Letterario*[1] one can see how he was working towards a pragmatic theory of his own that acknowledges a rigorous need for poetic form. Such an approach steers his poetry away from unmediated personal utterance and reveals a sympathetic engagement with the modernist notion of 'impersonality'.[2]

Bunting's indebtedness to Wordsworth, a poet for whom Pound had little sympathy, makes for a subtle and wider-ranging conversation and suggests that any account of Bunting's development as a poet needs to take English traditions into account. This is particularly germane when we come to discuss *Briggflatts*. Any critique of Bunting's poetic needs to measure the way in which he absorbed influences, including Persian influences, in order to fashion his own approach. Although Eliot chose not to publish Bunting's work in the 1950s because he felt it had too much of a Poundian imprint, it would be a mistake not to consider the limits of that influence. That Bunting was able to work within the traditions of English poetry, as well as take on board the experimental fiat of modernism, suggests a wider embrace that qualifies the modernist/anti-modernist division that hardened after the Second World War. Part of the excitement of engaging with Bunting's poetry is seeing how a modernist dynamic need not be incompatible with poetic sympathies nearer to home.

Bunting's experiences in Paris and Rapallo in the 1920s meant that his earlier work *was* marked by Poundian accents and underpinned by Poundian methodology. There were Eliotic cadences too and acknowledgement of Eliot's parodic strategies. The question of influence, however, is necessarily complicated. Taking the longer view, Michael Hamburger suggests that Pound's 'failure to "make it cohere" may well have something to do with his heterogeneous following in a world increasingly heterogeneous'.[3] Bunting's position on the inescapability of Pound is made clear in 'On the Fly-Leaf of Pound's Cantos' (*CP* 132).

Pound, Eliot and Bunting were all interested in the connection between poetry and music, a connection re-configured and revitalized by the French Symbolists: 'De la musique avant toute chose' proclaimed Paul Verlaine in 'Art Poétique' (1874). In an unpublished interview in 1976, Bunting argued that 'The Symbolist notions of sound, of poetry *as* sound, went further than Pound was prepared to go and were nearer to what I had in mind. I think that I have always been more concerned with the autonomy of the poem than any of the others – Pound, Williams or Zukofsky' (M&P 269). If Pound's legacy is wide-ranging and variegated 'one decidedly unifying factor in his work' argues Hamburger 'is his incomparable gift of *melopoeia*, to use his own term, a musical mastery and rightness that has failed him only where the message [...] seemed more important to him than the medium'.[4]

Neither for Pound nor Bunting was *melopoeia* a romantic surrender to the mellifluous. Yet the role of 'the ear' in poetry, and/or what Bunting described as 'an ear open to melodic analogies' is of particular significance. In the opening decades of the twentieth century this called for an awareness of contemporary music including the dissonant rhythms of jazz. Cacophony became as significant as harmony and Eliot's 'Shakespeherian Rag' catches that modish jazz note in *The Waste Land*. Bunting argues in his 'Statement':

> Poetry is seeking to make not meaning, but beauty; or if you insist on misusing words, its 'meaning' is of another kind, and lies in the relation to one another of lines and patterns of sound, perhaps harmonious, perhaps contrasting and clashing, which the hearer feels rather than understands. (S)

Bunting has made the importance of *hearing* poetry one of his key principles. 'Reading in silence' according to the poet 'is the source of half the misconceptions that have caused the public to distrust poetry' (S). The purpose of the 'Statement' is made clear in the opening paragraph:

> Poetry, like music, is to be heard. It deals in sound – long sounds and short sounds, heavy beats and light beats, the tone relations of vowels, the relations of consonants to one another which are like instrumental colour in music. Poetry lies dead on the page, until some voice brings it to life. (S)

It is important, however, that Bunting's pronouncements on the 'sounding' of poetry do not distract us from his compositional skills in general. As well as *melopoeia*, Pound had coined the terms *logopoeia* and *phanopoeia*. The first of these refers to 'the dance of intelligence among words' and the second is defined as the throwing of 'a visual image on the mind'. Zukofsky argued that 'The test of poetry is the range of pleasure it affords as sight, sound and intellection.'[5] Bunting's privileging of the sonic properties of poetry reveals an instinctive sympathy for poetry's oral traditions. By giving such importance to the musicality of poetry, which might seem both natural and uncontroversial, Bunting is staking out a pragmatic, even 'anti-theoretical' position. Quartermain, however, posits a more radical dynamic. Mindful of Bunting's Northumbrian provenance, he argues that in a marginalized culture 'priorities are always those of survival; so they are physical'. Bunting said: 'I like vowels that you can open your mouth and bawl' and that 'Poetry is just making noises [...] it's mouthfuls of air.'[6] By this reckoning, Bunting's privileging of sound over meaning side-steps the authority of written text. Distancing himself from both Pound and Zukofsky, Bunting maintained 'There is no excuse for literary criticism' (D). By making the analogy with music Bunting implies that poetry is a somatic experience which transcends interpretation. The 'unstopped ear' ultimately outwits the practice of academic exegesis: 'The theoreticians will follow the artist and fail to explain him' (S).

Bunting's analogy of poetry with music is never tantamount to saying that poetry *is* music and neither is Bunting guilty of vague bardic utterance. His pronouncements on 'beauty' are not a manifesto for meaninglessness. In conversation with Eric Mottram in 1975, Bunting maintained: 'I've never said that poetry consists *only* of sound. I said again and again that the *essential* thing is the sound. Without the sound, there isn't any poetry.'[7] Bunting was a formalist intimately concerned with structure, symmetry and rhythm, where sound and tonal change release their own meanings and where form is indivisible from content. This reminds us of Williams' notion, a reformulation of Zukofsky's pronouncements, that a poem is 'a small (or large) machine made of words' (SV 59). Bunting explains that he made the decision early 'that poetry should try to take over some of the new techniques that [he] only knew in music' (D). Out of this interest in music and out of a rigorous concern with composition, Bunting was drawn to the sonata.

The sonata as a musical form has evolved over time and is not without an elasticity of its own. It works by way of tonal contrast between a major and minor key, creating a sense of dialogue or dialectic, where the last movement, by way of return, takes us back to the initial key. The trajectory of a sonata is typically seen in these terms: Statement, Development/Exposition and Recapitulation. This provides a structured framework for a poetic enquiry that allows for focus, qualification and re-focus and which creates a synthesis emerging from an oppositional or binary dynamic. Bunting pointed out:

> I got off on the wrong foot trying to imitate Beethoven's sonatas, using extremely violent contrasts in tone and speed which don't actually carry well onto the page, and I had to puzzle about that for a while before I discovered it was better to go back to a simpler way of dealing with the two themes and to take the early or mid-eighteenth-century composers of sonatas – John Christian Bach and Scarlatti – as models to imitate. (*D*)

Bunting recognized the usefulness of the sonata's structure: 'where two themes which at first appear quite separate, and all the better if they're strongly contrasted ... gradually alter and weave together until at the end of your movement you've forgotten they are two themes, it's all one' (*SV* 258–9). Maintaining a unifying force, the poem-sonata allows for exploration as well as qualification.

By the time Bunting wrote *Briggflatts* sonata form had become integral to his poetic. In the 1920s he defined sonata form as 'The marriage of two contradictory spirits who both insist on talking stormily at the same time' (*M&P* 286). The poems discussed in this chapter were written between 1925 and 1935 and have a necessarily heuristic quality as the poet seeks to put technique into practice. The sonata was a useful model, to varying degrees a *shaping* structure, but ultimately these poems need to be judged not for how intricately they adhere to musical form but in the way in which an awareness of sonata form drives the poems. Pound argued that technique 'was the test of a man's sincerity' and the sonata provided Bunting with a technical apparatus that worked against loose romantic afflatus and inculcated an organizational coherence. 'A poem first and last', argues Makin in his analysis of Bunting's methodology, 'was a form made of sound' (*SV* 96).

VILLON

Born in Paris in 1431, the year Joan of Arc was burned at the stake, François Villon took his surname from his guardian and benefactor Guillaume de Villon, chaplain of Saint-Benoît-le-Bétourné.[8] Although there is a great deal of uncertainty about the biography of Villon, and much of it is gleaned from his poetry, we know that the poet took his *baccalauréat* from the University of Paris in 1449 and that the scholar-poet fell foul of the law in 1455 after he'd killed a priest in a fight. He was subsequently pardoned on the grounds that it was an act of self-defence yet in the same year he was implicated in a robbery at the College of Navarre. The poet left Paris and went on the run. He was later imprisoned by the Bishop of Orleans at Meung, but was set free for King Louis XI's celebratory progress through the town. It was in this period he worked on *Le Grand Testament*, his major work, which refers to his wanderings and travails. Villon found himself in prison again in 1462 charged with the robbery at the College of Navarre. He was released on condition that he repaid the money but in the same year was arrested for brawling. He found himself in the hands of the merciless Pierre de la Dehors who had the poet tortured and sentenced to be 'strangled and hanged on the gallows of Paris'.[9] Villon appealed to the Parliament for clemency and in January 1463 the Provost's sentence was annulled but the poet was banished from Paris for ten years 'in view of his bad character'. The poet left the city and slipped out of history. He was 32, not much older than Bunting himself when he embarked on his Villonesque redaction. Williams imagines that Villon was broken in spirit and health and might have died 'on a mat of straw in some cheap tavern; or in a cold, dank cell; or in a fight in some dark street [...] or perhaps as he always feared, on a gallows in a little town in France.'[10] François Rabelais entertained the idea that he came to England. Villon evidently took chances and risked his neck, a fifteenth-century poet of the streets whose 'contempt of law and love of women brought him down into the world of crooks and ponces'.[11] He was as colourful a character as Caravaggio or Jean Genet, affirming the subversive dynamic of poetry and ensuring his place in the long tradition of prison writing. One senses that the fifteenth-century Frenchman was seeking Bunting out.

If Dante was adept at creating a panoply of horrors, Villon was capable of withering satire; his wit 'is pointed but sly, his pathos poignant but controlled'.[12] Bunting was drawn to the candour of his poetic voice. Villon, in effect, helped the English poet develop that cultured, if sardonic, brio that drives much of his earlier work. The truculent young poet of the 1920s finds a confrère in the medieval Frenchman. Bunting's poem reveals a dynamic process of *creative* translation, adaptation and wholesale con- densation. *Villon*, a mere five pages, becomes a vibrant fragment, a 'blazing parchment' in its own right. It provided, at this early stage, a model of composition that served him well, where the pressure of the writing is predicated on cutting and conflating. Half a century later Bunting was advising students 'Cut out every word you dare. Do it again a week later, and again.'[13]

The opening of the three-movement poem broadcasts its intent by quoting and rendering ironic Clément Marot's somewhat patronizing assessment of Villon's work in his 1533 preface.[14] You can feel the freight of the quotation marks in the opening stanza:

> He whom we anatomized
> 'whose words we gathered as pleasant flowers
> and thought on his wit and how neatly he described things'
> speaks
> to us, hatching marrow,
> broody all night over the bones of a deadman.

> (CP 25)

The dead poet speaks to, or through, Bunting at the expense of Marot, whose name puns with 'marrow', and whose anodyne critique dilutes the dissident spirit of Villon. The opening manoeuvre of the poem signals Bunting's weariness of 'anatomization', or literary dissection – 'There is no excuse for literary criticism' – even as it reveals its own critical fiat. Bunting's poem demonstrates a self-referential awareness, not only by means of citation and allusion in its raids on the French text, but also in the manner it attends to its own creation as it wraps itself around sonata form. In effect, the poem becomes its own 'soundbox' whose penultimate line – 'How can I sing with my love in my bosom' – reminds us that the poem's argument is never un-connected to the tongue's curve 'in the ear', namely the poem's structure of sound or *melopoeia*.

The 'anatomized' poet draws attention to the *corporeality* of the piece or what Donald Davie described as 'the reek of the human'.[15] Bunting's purchase on Villon, both text and man, foregrounds the anatomy of the poem by inscribing its un-sentimental opening with 'the bones of a deadman'. Villon's poetry comes out of punitive personal experience where the body is typically the site of punishment and expiation. Bunting's *Villon* is not short of physical detail showing how chastisement is contiguous with the act of poetry: 'They took away the prison clothes/and on the frosty nights I froze'. The iconic denotations of art in the form of the Byzantine 'Emperor with the Golden Hands' whose metallic colour reminds us of handcuffs,[16] or the illuminated manuscripts of the English chronicler Matthew Paris, whose surname steers us back to Villon's city *and* anticipates the ravisher of Helen in Section Three, set up an opposition between art and life that nourishes the poem's wider conversation. The 'blazing parchment' created by Matthew Paris prefigures the fate of the 'good Lorraine' (Joan of Arc) whom the 'English burned at Rouen,/the day's bones whitening in centuries' dust' (CP 26). Bunting's poem operates as a treatise on power and oppression. The punitive and/or illicit collides with the poetic and hints at the dangers of poetic practice *per se*. The poet rides his luck or not. Bunting's *Villon* is neither a translation nor a version of the French text; rather it is a creative opportunity that is never historical in any narrow sense. 'The bones of a deadman' recall Eliot's 'rats' alley' where 'the dead men lost their bones' and just as it would be difficult to read *The Waste Land* without dwelling on the cultural crisis that arose after the 1914–18 war, Bunting's poem is likewise firmly located in the post-war years. Bunting's early sonatas scowl at the period in which they were written even as they return us to the medieval and classical worlds and consider the wider notion of mortality.

One of the tricks of *Villon* lies in the way in which the use of the first person conflates Villon with Bunting's poetic persona so that the Englishman's sympathetic identification with the French poet both masks and emboldens personal utterance. Bunting argues that his poetry comes out of experience but this is quite different from creating poems of naked autobiographi-cal declaration. Naïve biographical readings of his poems fail to recognize the extent to which Bunting has absorbed the modernist strategy of adopting personae and masks. It is useful to consider the relationship between Ezra Pound and Mauberley in *Hugh Selwyn Mauberley* or Eliot and Alfred Prufrock in *The Love Song of J. Alfred Prufrock*. The distance *and* collusion between the speaker and the poet set up their own particular resonances and bear out Oscar Wilde's quip that 'Man is least himself when he talks in his own person. Give him a mask, and he will tell you the truth.' In *Villon*, Bunting speaks through Villon and Villon speaks through Bunting, not only a breaking of bread with the dead, but a nod towards Eliot's argument about impersonality in 'Tradition and Individual Talent'. The poet should seek out a form of self-erasure, or 'escape from emotion', by writing with 'a historical sense' which 'compels a [poet] to write not merely with [their] own generation in his bones, but with a feeling that the whole of the literature of Europe from Homer onwards [...] has a simultaneous existence and composes a simultaneous order'. Eliot argues that the historical sense is 'nearly indispensable to anyone who would continue to be a poet beyond his twenty-fifth year', the exact age of Bunting when he wrote *Villon*.[17] Villon/Bunting creates both a symbiotic and stereo-effect that forges, in Eliot's words, 'a simultaneous order' which transcends the particulars of historical moment. Nevertheless, the pressure of biography, with its graphic accounts of prison experience, injects an inevitable force into Bunting's poem: '*Villon* ... is about my experiences, and Villon only supplies the decoration' (*SV* 27):

> In the dark in fetters
> on bended elbows I supported my weak back
> hulloing to muffled walls blank again
> unresonant. It was gone, is silent, is always silent.
> My soundbox lacks sonority.

> (*CP* 25)

Bunting employs a variety of metrical and prosodic strategies that take their bearings from Villon but which also allow greater variation and experimentation. Variable stanzas harden into Gautier-like quatrains in the first section before moving into a single-block piece in the second. Section Three begins with a long enjambed passage free of punctuation where the shorter line holds sway. Add to this the violent juxtapositions and sudden gear-changes, as well as the skilful alliteration together with the mosaic of allusions/quotations, and we begin to get a feel for the risk-taking audacity of the piece. In the first section, the use of repetition and internal rhyme hold up the rhythm of the writing to create a bleak, controlling symmetry:

> To the right was darkness and to the left hardness
> below hardness darkness above
> at the feet darkness at the head partial hardness.
>
> (CP 25)

Descriptions of Villon/Bunting in a prison cell continue in Section Two. The second line refers quite specifically to the Bishop of Orleans' imprisonment of Villon:

> Let his days be few and let
> his bishoprick [bishop-*prick*] pass to another,
> for he fed me on carrion and on a dry crust,
> mouldy bread that his dogs had vomited,
> I lying on my back in the dark place, in the grave,
> fettered to a post in the damp cellarage.

Bunting is writing out of his experiences in Wormwood Scrubs or one of the military prisons in which he'd been incarcerated:

> there are no dancers, no somersaulters now,
> only bricks and bleak black cement and bricks,
> only the military tread and the snap of the locks.
>
> (CP 27)

Now the longer line breaks into rhyming couplets, quickening the tempo:

> Mine was a threeplank bed whereon
> I lay and cursed the weary sun.
> They took away the prison clothes
> and on the frosty nights I froze.
> I had a Bible where I read
> that Jesus came to raise the dead –
> I kept myself from going mad
> by singing an old bawdy ballad
> and birds sang on my windowsill
> and tortured me till I was ill.
>
> (CP 27)

If sleep is 'the prisoner's release', poetic imagination brings a balm of its own. Reviewing Joseph Conrad's *The Rover* for *The Transatlantic Review* in 1924, Bunting describes a psychological process that has some bearing on *Villon*:

> I read *Romance* for the first time in the solitude of an English prison. [...] *Romance* was a real book, a book written by man and not by the heavy finger of God. In that emptiness, where no new thing ever enters, it took possession of my eyes and ears. My cell grew full of aromatic bales, fading into the shadows of Don Ramon's warehouse; Thomas Castro walked with me around the patch of rotting cabbage-stalks that was our exercise ground; even Seraphina visited me occasionally, keeping modestly to the dark places, an indistinct but sympathetic form. It was all amazingly concrete. (*PBB* 150–1)

If the singing birds are a form of torture in *Villon*, the impure ballad brings relief not by means of holy visitation but through sexual fantasy, which in the darkness of a prison cell might be rather more efficacious. If Seraphina had been Bunting's heavenly visitor, he now co-opts Villon's Archipiada from the *Ballade des Dames du Temps Jadis* as another manifestation of physical consolation: 'but Archipiada came to me/and comforted my cold body'. Yet the mythological stakes are raised by the reference to Circe who 'lay with me in that dungeon for a year/ making a silk purse from an old sow's ear/till Ronsard put a thimble on her tongue' (*CP* 27–8). The Homeric reference recalls Odysseus' year-long entrapment with the sorceress/weaver who had turned his men into swine. Bunting has alluded to this somewhat obliquely in the first section: 'eyes lie and this *swine's fare* bread and water/makes my head wuzz' (my italics); and here in Section Two he pushes home the allusion by extending the 'silk purse' idiom. Bunting is working between texts with some agility and the bravura is capped by the reference to the court poet Pierre de Ronsard, a near contemporary of Marot and a leading poet of the French *Pléiade*, who in the spirit of the Renaissance set about classicizing French poetry. Ronsard's placing of a thimble on Circe's tongue not only silences the 'excellent utterer' of the mind with an accoutrement from her own workshop no less, it signifies a closing down of Villon's subversive, irreverential verse. Bunting provides a broad literary history at the moment he attends to the minutiae of the poem. If he scorns the *haut en bas* regard of the courtly Ronsard, he lets the classical narrative heighten the poem's emotional pitch.

After his sojourn with Circe, Odysseus descends into the underworld. Whereas the next passage springs the reader from the 'damp cellerage', the 'underworld' or 'inferno' has by now been perfectly constructed. The long lines in the second part of Section Two colonize the page as Bunting transforms historical-mythological-environmental matter into contemporary relevance before returning to Villon's plaintive text at the end of the section. Bunting describes the modern malaise of fact-pinching bureaucracy and soulless utilitarianism where, in a reductive taxonomy, 'the stars are all named', 'the white moon' runs to a schedule and where, by means of a bold ecological/mythological conceit, the narrator declares 'They have melted the snows from Erebus' (*CP* 28). The pressure of allusiveness is superbly charged. Archipiada, Villon's idiosyncratic invention, or seeming mis-prision, is now sought by private detectives and this notion of surveillance takes us to the French policeman Alphonse Bertillon (1854–1914) who created a pseudo-scientific method of identify-ing criminals called anthropometrics which involved the measur-ing and recording of physical characteristics. The double apostrophe, '(O anthropometrics!)', and later 'O Bertillon!', renders ironic the grubby and questionable procedures of the dubious law enforcer. Much of Bertillon's work was carried out in La Santé Prison and it's not unreasonable to imagine that Bunting himself was processed and archived in some kind of anthropometric system: 'Colour of hair? of eyes? of hands? O Bertillon!' (*CP* 28). The golden hands of the emperor are recalled in the subsequent question 'How many golden prints on the smudgy page?', which now enacts a crossover from police procedure to the teacher-like roll-call that follows.[18] The lines at the end of Section Two have a particular valency:

> Homer? Adest. Dante? Adest.
> Adsunt omnes, omnes et
> Villon.
> Villon?
> Blacked by the sun, washed by the rain,
> hither and thither scurrying as the wind varies.

> (*CP* 28)

Bunting acknowledges Homer and Dante, whose literary presence is central to the *Cantos* and *The Waste Land*, and thus nods again to Eliot's argument regarding historical consciousness in 'Tradition and the Individual Talent'. The Latin (Adest,

Adsunt) can be translated as 'here' or 'present', reminding us, in fact, of a schoolboy responding to a teacher's register. The line-break after 'omnes et' creates a tactical hesitation before the eye moves down to Villon, and the drama is enforced by the repetition of his name which is followed by that tell-tale question mark – Villon? Bunting both posits and queries the role of the French poet in the literary canon and the question mark (present or not?) reminds us of Villon's disappearance from history. Suter argues that 'by comparing himself with Villon, Bunting may also have discovered [...] the sense of his own artistic inadequacy, a major theme of his poems.'[19] The question might now be framed: Homer, Dante, Villon, (Bunting)?

The end of Section Two creates, at first hearing, a peculiarly lyrical note until we realize that 'Blacked by the sun, washed by the rain,/hither and thither scurrying as the wind varies' is a translation of the lines that Villon wrote on the eve of his anticipated execution in the *Ballade des Pendus*. The lines suggest the swaying bodies of hanged men, a fifteenth-century rendering of Billie Holiday's lynching song 'Strange Fruit'. The lay-out of the lines forces a laceration or jump in the text, disclosing the shape of the gallows themselves, as well as the dangling form of the hanged man. The question mark has now become a half-noose:

> Homer? Adest. Dante? Adest.
> Adsunt onmes, omnes et
> Villon.
> Villon?

> (CP 28)

Bunting has negotiated and re-created the infernal with the same energy as Pound in the 'Hell Cantos', which take their bearings from Homer's *Nekuia* and Dante's *Inferno*. If Dante is the divine creator of the infernal, the trajectory of Bunting's work demonstrates how skilfully he takes the reader into that selfsame region. We can see how Bunting, from *Villon* onwards, engages with the modernist tropes of profanity and spiritual crisis which he colours with his own brand of vitriol and scatological gesture.

Villon gives us:

> Je congnois que povres et riches,
> Sages et folz prestres et laiz,

> Nobles, villains larges et chiches,
> Petiz et grans, et beaulx et laiz,
> Dames a rebrassez colletz,
> De quelconque condicion,
> Portans atours et bourreletz –
> Mort saisit sans exepcion.[20]

Bunting takes Villon's eight-line stanzas from *Le Testament* and tackles the theme of mortality with relish. In the second half of Section One, he employs a set of octosyllabic quatrains (abab), as well as slipping in that penultimate tercet which houses the poem's statement regarding impermanence. The poem's basic philosophy is laid out:

> Remember, imbeciles and wits,
> sots and ascetics, fair and foul,
> young girls with little tender tits,
> that DEATH is written over all.

and

> Abelard and Eloise,
> Henry the Fowler, Charlemagne,
> Genée, Lopokova, all these
> die, die in pain.
>
> (*CP* 26)

Bunting steps out of the fifteenth century, the poem is never really in any other age than its own, hauls the past into the present and trawls a generously populated hell containing General Grant and General Lee, Patti and Florence Nightingale. In Eliot's 'Marina' (1929), 'Those who sharpen the tooth of the dog meaning/Death' become 'insubstantial, reduced by a wind'; in *Villon* 'our doom/is, to be sifted by the wind because *We are less permanent than thought*' (my italics, *CP* 27). The statement is enunciated in the only three-line stanza of this section, the lost line itself inscribing evanescence. The bones of a deadman have now become the focus of our meditation, a rhythmic *danse macabre*, or a relentless chain of *memento mori*, and not without a hint of Boethius' *The Consolation of Philosophy*.[21]

In Section Three the poem returns to the poetic crisis evinced in Section One: 'My soundbox lacks sonority'. The weight of this statement is significant in a poem which subscribes to musical form. After Villon's 'hanging lines' at the end of Section Two, the

36

third section opens with a lyrical, incremental passage motored by 4-stress lines that takes us via 'olive trees' to 'the beauty of Helen' and further Homeric narrative. Bunting uses a Mediterranean *topos* (Rapallo) to take us back to Paris – city *and* mythological figure – and by doing so he neatly lays down the key geographical coordinates of his apprenticeship years. The passage, now free from the constraints of punctuation, yet perfectly modulated in its delivery, elides with that emblematic statement regarding poetic strategy. 'Precision clarifying vagueness' is a neat reformulation of Imagist principles,[22] where the 'chisel voice' not only looks ahead to the opening section of *Briggflatts* but reaffirms the adamantine quality of Poundian poetics.[23] Bunting's poetry habitually comments on the art of poetry:

> precision clarifying vagueness;
> boundary to a wilderness
> of detail; chisel voice
> smoothing the flanks of noise;
> catalytic making whisper and whisper
> run together like two drops of quicksilver;
> factor that resolves
>   unnoted harmonies;
> name of the nameless;
>   stuff that clings
> to frigid limbs
>   more marble hard
> than girls imagined by Mantegna ...

(CP 29)

In Section One we are told that 'Vision is lies' and the soundbox/ vision binary now effects a resolution by *noting* the 'unnoted harmonies' and collapsing them into 'the silence of a single note' where 'The sea has no renewal. No forgetting,/no variety of death'. The reference to the painter Mantegna underscores a lapidary poetic whose marbled imagery combines with the poem's sound-shape to achieve a final synthesis. This leaves us with the quirky codetta:

> How can I sing with my love in my bosom?
> Unclean, immature and unseasonable salmon.

(CP 29)

Hesitant Troubadour, Bunting has made poetry into song, has

rediscovered the sonority of his 'soundbox', has transcended the confines of his cell by finding his poetic voice. Yet the final line, with its self-accusatory negatives, and where 'salmon' half-rhymes with 'bosom' in quixotic embrace, underscores the heuristic if, ultimately, gnomic nature of *Villon*. This flourish at the last leads Cox to argue that the poem 'finishes with a mocking kick of the heels, a twirl typical of the twenties, which slights the poet's own achievement and puts the poem back into its own situation'.[24]

ATTIS: OR, SOMETHING MISSING AND THE WELL OF LYCOPOLIS

Although I will be considering each of these poems on its own merits, there's a usefulness in considering *Attis* and *The Well* together. Neither poem is without its textual complications. Whereas *Villon* allows the reader to get a purchase on the poem through the original French and/or the respective biographies of the poets, both *Attis* and *The Well* might be considered as modernist exercises in mythopoetry. Written in 1931 and 1935 respectively, they are clearly cognizant of Pound's earlier *Cantos* as well as Eliot's *The Waste Land* (1922). Both these poets had deliberately developed a mythological reflex in their writing. Neither should we ignore the significance of James Joyce's *Ulysses* (1922). In 1923 Eliot had written an assessment of Joyce's modernist novel in his essay 'Ulysses, Order and Myth'. Eliot argues that Joyce has created a parallel between contemporaneity and antiquity, so pursuing a method which others should pursue after him. Eliot concludes by saying 'Instead of narrative method, we may now use the mythical order.'[25] Although he is addressing the form of the modern novel, Eliot's essay not only describes the methodology of *The Waste Land*, it posits the greater usefulness of the mythopoeic method over the randomness of meaningless particulars, and is thereby suggesting the challenges and limits of literary realism. Eliot's classicizing drive, not uninfluenced by the anthropological enquiries of Frazer's *The Golden Bough* and Weston's *From Ritual to Romance*, reveals a craving for order in the face of contemporary flux and gives us notice of the poet's authoritarian agenda.

Neil Corcoran argues that Eliot's *Four Quartets* (1944) 'brings Modernist free verse and Mallarméan symbolism to their ultimate pitch in English writing, even in the act of chastising their inadequacy'.[26] There is a suggestion here that Eliot who had been instrumental in bringing one strand of modernist poetics to fruition in *The Waste Land* was now, in this later poem, intimating the limits of that project. High Modernism had found its most forceful literary expression in the decades before and after the First World War and both *The Waste Land* and *Ulysses* were published in 1922. As early as 1942, the American poet-critic Randall Jarrell was asking in 'The End of the Line' whether anyone would have 'believed that modernism would collapse so fast?'[27] Yet the chronological bracketing of any literary-cultural movement is necessarily problematic, and equally so the charting of its legacies and continuities.

Both *Attis* and *The Well* reveal a set of poetic strategies that are emblematic of modernist endeavour. Any reading of the poems would recognize that both texts are larded with allusions, citations and/or 'quotations'. These include references, *inter alia*, to Milton, Eliot, Cino Da Pistoia and Villon. Not only do the poems demonstrate a parodying, even scarifying, vein, they show how Bunting's habit of translation continues to inform his writing. The poet's interest in Lucretius, Catullus and Horace, not to mention a typically modernist engagement with Dante, is variously threaded into the poems. Their very arrangement, where fragments, mythological and otherwise, are marshalled into a unifying whole by way of juxtaposition rather than linear drive, indicates a general adherence to 'mythical order'. Bunting employs mythological narrative to critique the contemporary so that tropes of paralysis and degradation are brought into sharp relief by the ironic handling of classical narrative. In both poems there's a great deal of erudition that's both scholarly and parodic and which, at first sight, would seem to draw little on immediate personal experience in the way of *Villon, Aus Dem Zweiten Reich* or the later poems.

Both poems are concerned with the creative anxiety that underpins poetic creation. The fear of failure forms the basis of the creative act itself so that Bunting reflects on the complexity of creativity in the very process of creating. One might read these poems as cultural commentaries at a particularly significant moment in European history. A decade or so after the First World War and less than a decade before the outbreak of the Second World War – and now in the aftermath of the Wall Street Crash of 1929 – the poet holds his poetic nerve even as he writes about loss of nerve and burgeoning cynicism. These are the years of hardening ideologies and political crises. Bunting's perspectives are refracted through a collage of mythological narratives as he works his way through the influences of Pound and Eliot. He takes the measure of his own poetic abilities as he threads a meta-poetic dimension into the poetry itself. John Seed argues:

> Bunting's poetry of the 1930s is haunted by this sense of its own inadequacy, its inability to integrate the pressures of external reality and subjective feeling, its failure to integrate the pressures of external reality and subjective feeling, its failure either to achieve the formal perfection of art or to serve urgent human needs in a period of acute social crisis. In the words of Holderlin, 'wozu Dichter in durftiger Zeit?' What are poets for in a time of need?[28]

Bunting pointed out that 'It certainly wouldn't be easy to write a synopsis' of *Attis* but 'I think it's really fairly plain for all that, if the reader doesn't spend time and energy looking for a nice logical syllogistic development which isn't there' (*PBB* 159). The poem's scaffolding seems to have been taken down in part which not only reveals a self-referential quality but also provides a masterclass on mythopoeic strategy. *Attis* is prefaced by an epigraph from Catallus' 'Carmen 63' which refers directly to the myth that stands at the heart of the poem. Although Bunting takes his bearings from Catallus' account, there are various versions and in Book II of *De Rerum Natura*, Lucretius refers to the cult of Cybele (Earth Goddess or Great Mother) whose most elevated priestly followers have mutilated themselves.[29] From Catullus we learn that Attis, a youthful Phrygian leader, together with his companions, castrate themselves in a state of religious frenzy before the mountain (Dindyma) dedicated to Cybele. When the religious ecstasy has abated Attis despairs at what he has done: 'Cybele, hearing him, sends one of her lions to the shore where Attis is looking toward his fatherland, to drive him back among the mountain pines as her subservient eunuch' (*PBB* 160).

Instead of the *l'homme moyen sensuel* whose appetites are considered variously by Larkin et al. in the poetry of the 1950s and 1960s, Bunting uses the story of Attis to satirize the conceits and anxieties of the *entre les deux guerres* man. One might choose to read these early poems of Bunting as a fragmented conversation about the crisis of masculinity in the early twentieth century and the crisis of the male poet not infrequently abandoned by the female muse. In effect, we have to wait until *Briggflatts* to see how Bunting addresses the trauma of 'discarded love'. The emasculated Attis, denoted in Catullus' Latin epigraph, is now transformed into an unedifying contemporary portrait. This might be an ageing version of Prufrock, effeminate, going to seed:

> Out of puff
> noonhot in tweeds and gray felt,
> tired of appearance and
> disappearance;
> warm obese frame limp with satiety;
> slavishly circumspect at sixty;
> he spreads over the ottoman
> scanning the pictures and table trinkets.

> > (*CP* 30)

Bunting's emasculated modern man 'regrets that brackish/train of the huntress/driven into slackening fresh,' which is

> > expelled when the
> > > estuary resumes
> > colourless potability;
> > > wreckage that drifted
> > in drifts out.

> > (*CP* 30)

There's an echo, perhaps, of Eliot's 'departed nymphs' who have skipped away from Edmund Spenser's mythic Thames, leaving the river littered with 'empty bottles, sandwich papers' and 'cigarette ends'. In Bunting's poem, the hunting motif, with all its heroic and classical implications, is sustained in the fourth stanza where the image of 'hounds trooping around hooves' is now undercut by a contemporary (aristocratic) staccato interjection: '*Voice*: Have you seen the/fox? Which way did he go? he go?' (*CP* 31). Instead of the grandeur of the opening of Eliot's 'Fire Sermon', the speaker remembers 'deep mud and leafmould somewhere' and the Northumbrian Cheviot Hills with 'their heatherbrown flanks and white cap' become a point

41

of reference. The first section of *Attis*, characterized by variegated and changing form, ends by reinforcing the environmental concern we saw in the second section of *Villon*. The sterility trope, which is central to *The Waste Land*, is here reconfigured. Cybele, 'Mother of Gods' and 'Mother of Eunuchs', gives and takes in equal measure: 'Landscape' is blessed with 'superabundance' or blighted with 'parsimonious/ soil'. Section One concludes with two neat four-lined stanzas which reveal a psalmic quality as well as reminding us of Cybele's destructive agency:

> From her brooks sweat. Hers corn and fruit.
>   Earthquakes are hers too. Ravenous animals
>   are sent by her. Praise her and call her
> Mother and Mother of Gods and Eunuchs.

> (CP 31)

The opening of Section Two steps away from mythical narrative and provides the reader with a parenthetical signpost: (*Variations on a theme by Milton*.) The droll opening lines – 'I thought I saw my late wife (a very respectable woman)/coming from Bywell churchyard with a handful of raisins' (CP 31) – alludes to Milton's sonnet 'Methought I Saw My Late Espoused Saint'. Milton's sonnet reverences his deceased wife by comparing her with the mythological heroine Alcestis ('Love, sweetness, goodness, in her person shined'). Bunting reveals a debunking reflex: 'I was not pleased, it is shocking to meet a ghost, so I cut her/and went and sat amongst the rank watergrasses by the Tyne' (CP 31). Again, the lines draw us directly to *The Waste Land*. Instead of the Smyrna merchant 'with a pocket full of currants', Bunting's speaker holds 'a handful of raisins' and whereas Eliot's speaker sits down by the water of Leman to weep, Bunting's Northumbrian speaker chooses the River Tyne. Bunting's intertextual dynamic is both subtle and effective. Not only is he parodying Eliot's literary interventions, but his allusion to 'Methought [...]' also evokes Milton's *Paradise Lost* which, in turn, adds its weight to the eschatological enquiries within Bunting's poem. The prose calm of the opening lines switches to the exclamatory rhythms of the fatal dance – 'Centrifugal tutus! Sarabands!' – soon descending into religious 'frenzy' and the moment of mutilation: (Andante.... ....

Prestissimo!). The reference to 'turbulent Orfeo' (the medieval Orpheus) sustains the mythopoeic and underpins Bunting's continuing engagement with underworld imagery (*CP* 31).

In the next passage we are introduced to Tesiphone's and Alecto's 'capillary orchestra' by means of 'muted violins'. In a poem that acknowledges sonata form, Bunting lays out musical instruments as well as musical motifs, prefiguring similar operations in *Briggflatts*. By referring to the Furies and their exhortation to the Medusa, Bunting takes us into the ninth Canto of Dante's *Inferno*. In Canto 8, the narrator has learnt that if he were to follow Virgil into the city of Dis there would be no certainty of return, generating an understandable attack of dread: 'Pensa, lettor, se io mi sconfortai/nel soun de le parole maladette,/ché non credetti ritornaci mai.'[30] Canto 9 opens, in fact, with the narrator beset by cowardice – 'Quel color che viltà di fuor mi pinse'[31] – and some fifty or so lines later the Furies call on Medusa to turn him into stone: 'Vegna Medusa: sì 'l farem di smalto'. Bunting borrows from Dante and gives us:

> VENGA MEDUSA
> VENGA
> MEDUSA SÌ L'FAREM DI SMALTO
> *Send for Medusa: we'll enamel him!*

(*CP* 32)

In the *Inferno*, Virgil covers the eyes of the narrator and the 'un-dead' poet is spared the transformation. Yet moral petrifaction, loss of creative nerve and incipient despair permeate both *Attis* and *The Well*. Bunting conflates his own anxieties as a young poet wrestling with the influences of Pound/Eliot with the wider consciousness of European crisis. Writing in what Auden described as a 'low dishonest decade', Bunting draws on modernist tropes of cultural and sexual crisis. Prufrockian anxiety – 'Do I dare?' – seeps into the more abrasive discourse of *Attis* whose 'Something Missing' transcends Prufrock's moral pusillanimity. *The gorgon's method* becomes an analogue of Eliot's Dantean description of city workers flowing over London Bridge: 'I had not thought death had undone so many.' *Attis* takes us back to the metropolis whose morning light has temporarily banished the private (ghostly) nocturnal world, where 'The banality of daylight shrivels one's private and nameless, dreams' (*SV* 84–5):

> *The gorgon's method:*
> In the morning
> clean streets welcomed light's renewal,
> patient, passive to the weight of buses
> thundering like cabinet ministers
> over a lethargic populace.
> Streets buffeted thin soles at midday,
> streets full of beggars.
> Battered, filthily unfortunate streets
> perish, their ghosts are wretched
> in the mockery of lamps.
>
> (*CP* 32)

If the classical gods and their friends 'skulk/from impotence in light's/opacity' the night shows them in stalking mode:

> (VENGA MEDUSA)
> passionately.
>
> (*CP* 33)

The collapse of the heroic is played out in the final stanza of Section Two where Polymnia, the muse of poetry and sacred song, is now reduced to running a café in Reno. In an intertextual side-step, Bunting rhymes Reno with Cino (Cino da Pistoia), a contemporary and friend of Dante as well as the subject of an early poem by Pound ('Cino'). In Pound's poem we find the interjection – 'Oh, eh, Cino' – as the medieval poet sings 'women in three cities'. Forde argues that [Bunting's] aside to Cino da Pistoia 'may remind a few readers of Rossetti's criticism of Cino's elaborate and mechanical tone of complaint which hardly reads like the expression of true love' (*PBB* 164). Bunting gives us:

> Polymnia
> keeps a café in Reno.
> Well, (eh, Cino?)
>
> (*CP* 33)

In Polymnia's café, modern man declares

> I dare no longer raise my eyes
> on any lass
> seeing what one of them has done to me.

Section Three, which is rather appropriately described as a *pastorale ariosa* in *falsetto*, takes us directly back to the story of Attis. Bunting conflates various versions; the pine reference recalls Attis' transformation into a fir tree. The opening line, where 'stave' is both musical notation and tree wood, acknowledges the metamorphosis. The 'stiffening' Attis is now imbued with painful irony:

> What mournful stave, what bellow shakes the grove?
> O, it is Attis grieving for his testicles!
> Attis stiffening amid the snows
> and the wind whining through his hair and fingers!
>
> (*CP* 33)

In Catullus' 'Carmen 63' the emasculated Attis remembers his prowess as an athlete; here Bunting modernizes: 'I also won the 14 carat halfhunter goldwatch/at the annual sports and flower-show./The young girls simpered when I passed.' Now he is out of a job and would 'like to be lady's maid/to Dindyma' (*CP* 33). The 'procreative energy' which is yearned for by 'Pensive geldings' not only becomes a scornful analysis of contemporary malaise (both lack of Prufrockian daring in *The Love Song of J. Alfred Prufrock* and impotence in the Fisher King narrative in *The Waste Land*) but also a continuation of the conversation regarding poetic integrity. The poet's own sense of creative crisis wraps itself round his critique of modernity. Arguably, Bunting is also considering the representational challenges of modernist poetry, where the mimetic gives way to the mythopoeic. These early poems are hardly risk-free, are occasionally abstruse and not always fully achieved. The analogy of male potency with creativity is typically phallocentric and recalls Pound's description of 'the phallus or spermatozoid charging, head-on [into] female chaos'.[32] The 'castrated' poet can no longer poeticize. Fear of castration, and castration is alluded to again in *The Well*, suggests Bunting's Oedipal struggle with his 'modernist' fathers.[33] Making a somewhat different point, Seed argues:

> It is tempting to trace the tension between sensual delight and self-disgust, and this overwhelming sense of guilt and failure to deep inner conflicts between his hereditary Quaker Puritanism and his wild Bohemian lifestyle, between the civic responsibilities of the

Liberal-radical professional of his family background and the idleness and narcissism in the conventional picture of the artist.[34]

In Section Three, we learn that Attis has not only lost his erstwhile athleticism but is now unable to sing the 'ithyphallic hymns' used in Bacchanalian celebration of the phallus. In a knowing display of creative self-abnegation the speaker tells us:

> I have forgotten most of the details,
>> most of the names,
>> and the responses to
>> the ithyphallic hymns:
>> forgotten the syntax.

(CP 34)

Catching hold of the vernacular in Eliot's 'Pub Scene', or in Polymnia's café no less, Attis exclaims:

> (Oh Sis!
> I've been 'ad!
> I've been 'ad proper!)

(CP 34)

The aspirated "ad' is freighted and far-reaching in a poem about 'Something Missing'. Cybele's bewitching of Attis is a good example of man messing up. Yet the castrated priests of Cybele might traditionally have sought consolation in Elysium; 'shall we be whole in Elysium?', Attis asks anxiously. Now he is garlanded with early Christian symbols – roses, myrtles and peacocks – and Cybele's response is less than comforting: 'The Peacock's knavery/keeps you in slavery' (CP 35). One wonders whether Bunting's non-dogmatic Quaker background encourages him to draw on Lucretius' atheistic attitude to critique the jiggery-pokery of dangerous ritual. The couplet at the end of *Villon* is determinedly ludic; Cybele's response to the hapless Attis now dovetails into a pointed endnote:

> Attis his embleme:
> *Nonnulla deest.*

(CP 35)

The Latin tag – something's missing – might hint at the negation of deity itself (*deest* is almost an anagram of *deus*) thus setting up a subtle counter-reading of 'The Return', Pound's invocation of the pagan gods. Something missing ultimately refers to more than Attis' broken manhood. It fashions a vitriolic complaint about contemporary culture and integrity in a wider sense and explores, variously, the poet's relationship with his art. Bunting continues these enquiries in *The Well of Lycopolis*.

THE WELL OF LYCOPOLIS

Bunting described *Attis* as a 'sonatina'. *The Well* is a sonata in four sections. Less compact and rather less unified than both *Attis* and *Villon*, it can be seen as an early attempt to seek out the more ambitious structure we find in *The Spoils* and the five-part *Briggflatts*. Fisher enjoys its 'eloquent scruffiness'.[35] *The Well* is a bleak and occasionally eccentric piece of writing which, nevertheless, releases its own particular resonances.

In Bunting's translation of Rudaki, the aged speaker laments: 'All the teeth ever I had are worn down and fallen out' (*CP* 155). Decay and decline, both sexual and generic is contrasted with happier, youthful times when 'the title-page of [the old man's] book was Love and Poetry'. Love and Poetry are the main constituents of these early sonatas, though in *The Well* the formula is re-worked into 'Infamous poetry, abject love' and 'Abject poetry, infamous love' (*CP* 42–3). If sexual politics are mythologized in *Attis*, mythological recourse in this later poem barely disguises Bunting's deepening state of personal dejection. The Buntings had left Rapallo for Tenerife at the end of 1933 for economic reasons. Yet their new reality made the situation worse. Much of their income came in the form of handouts from Marian's parents. The impecunious life was demoralizing, the climate oppressive. Bunting wrote to Pound: 'Nothing but a tentpeg through the skull could distract me more completely than the sort of life we've had to lead' (*SV* 75). In 1936 Bunting writes: 'Escaped from Tenerife (formerly Isla del Infierno)' (*SV* 81). The Buntings' marriage came to an end soon after.

The Latin epigraph to *The Well* comes from a footnote in Edward Gibbons' *Decline and Fall of the Holy Roman Empire* and suggests that a potion from the well takes away virginity (*PBB* 172). Not only is the pre-lapsarian banished from the start, the writing works as a valediction to sexual and creative fulfilment.

The second epigraph comes from the opening of Villon's *Les Regrets de la Belle Heaulmière*. The old woman's complaint against the irreversibility of time, typically forthright in the Villonesque manner and at moments recalling something of the cantankerous Wife of Bath, is now redirected through the mouth of an ageing Venus whose language is both contemporary and demotic.

> I had them all on a string at one time,
> lawyers, doctors, business-men:
> there wasn't a man alive but would have given
> all he possessed
> for what they wont take now free for nothing.
> I turned them down,
> I must have had no sense,
> for the sake of a shifty young fellow:
> whatever I may have done at other times
> on the sly
> I was in love then and no mistake;
> and him always knocking me about
> and only cared for my money.

(CP 39)

The modernity of Bunting's Mother Venus is nuanced by her claim that she is 'a British subject', reminding us that her mythological provenance is Paphos, Cyprus. Her modern self is reinforced by her borrowings from the Vaudevillian performer Sophie Tucker, also known as 'The Last of the Red Hot Mamas' (*CP* 225). The focus is now the First World War and Venus remembers:

> kids carrying the clap to school under their pinnies,
> studying Belgian atrocities in the Sunday papers
> or the men pissing in the backstreets; and grown women
> sweating their shifts sticky at the smell of khaki.

(CP 40)

Venus fetches up at Polymnia's:

> glowering stedfastly at the lukewarm
> undusted grate grim with cinders
> never properly kindled.

(CP 40)

In these less than salubrious surroundings the muse of poetry is still able to parody Eliotic utterance, 'Time is, was, has been', before she too takes up the mantle of the Belle Heaulmière:

> Blotched belly, slack buttock and breast,
> there's little to strip for now.
> A few years makes a lot of difference.

(CP 41)

To these 'devoutly worshipped ladies', degraded icons of Love and Poetry, a 'libation of flat beer' is offered with the proviso they 'retch cold bile' (CP 41). If Bunting has been skilful in parodying Eliot, the middle part of The Well now has Bloomsbury in its sights and it is useful to consider Makin's observation regarding that 'group of poems written between 1924 and 1935' in which Bunting would appear to be commenting on 'the indeterminate sexual identities of Bloomsbury' creating, in turn, 'a metaphor for cowardice in poetry' (SV 82). Polymnia, with slapstick risibility, is instructed to look upon:

> the sleek, slick lads treading gingerly between the bedpots,
> stripped buff-naked all but their hats to raise,
> and nothing rises but the hats;
> smooth, with soft steps, *ambiguoque voltu.*[36]

(CP 42)

Horace's 'ambiguous face' slips us into the mythological narrative of Daphnis and Chloe, their virginal love at ironic counterpoint with the polluting power of Lycopolis. Catching hold of Eliotic cadence, Bunting skewers Bloomsbury with geographical coordinates:

> We have laid on Lycopolis water.
> The nights are not fresh
> between High Holborn and the Euston Road,
> nor the days bright even in summer
> nor the grass of the squares green.

(CP 42)

Bunting manages several narratives simultaneously. He re-invests in mythological narrative of various kinds to frame his critique of London/Europe between the wars in order to reveal a particular animus towards the self-regarding, precious and privileged coterie of Bloomsbury. D. H. Lawrence satirized Lady Ottoline Morrell in *Women in Love* and we can see how

Bunting, who came to know something of Bloomsbury between the wars, had little affinity with the group. He complained that the Bloomsbury Group 'were all of that well-to-do middle class, bordering on country gentry who felt that if you couldn't afford to live in Bloomsbury [...] well, poor devil, there wasn't much to be expected of you. Then also, their patronage was something I didn't like the smell of.'[37] Pound had provided an assessment of contemporary English culture in *Hugh Selwyn Mauberley*, and there's no shortage of vitriol in his description of the British Empire in post-1918 decline. These early pieces by Bunting constitute a kind of 'metropolitan shudder', where the metropolis supplies its own infernal consciousness. Bunting, whose northern provenance created a necessary marginalizing effect, wrote to Dorothy Pound in 1954: 'Our only hope for our children is to destroy uniformity, centralisation, big states and big cities.'[38] Bunting's cultural-political alignments were complicated. If he had no time for Bloomsbury, he was dismayed by 'the rightward political turn' of Yeats, Eliot and Pound, all of which 'contributed to Bunting's sense of isolation and of profound uncertainty [...] at critically disentangling the political ambiguities of the modernist aesthetic in the 1930s.'[39] He was no more comfortable with the young left-wing poets of the 1930s – Auden, Spender, MacNiece et al. – who operated within metropolitan literary circles with ease.

'Infamous poetry, abject love' which becomes 'Abject poetry, infamous love' might serve as the poem's motto. Not only does it feed on the poet's own personal circumstances, but it also echoes the mordant, jaundiced spirit of Pound's *Mauberley*. 'Hell's constellations' not only recall *The gorgon's method* in *Attis*, but they also remind us of Bunting's personal hell on the Isla di Infierno and look ahead to the Dantean conclusion of the poem. In *The Love Song of J. Alfred Prufrock* the women 'come and go talking about Michelangelo'. Here, 'women's faces/blank or trivial' slip scatalogically into 'tweet, tweet, twaddle,/tweet, tweet, twat' and 'Squalid acquiescence in the cast-offs/of reputed poetry' (*CP* 43). Attis now collides with Bellerophon, another castrate from mythology, who becomes a representative of grub street – 'a livery hack, a gelding' – all 'mansuetude and indifference', and the poet could well be thinking of his own journalistic experiences. Bunting's contempt of 'cunnilingual law' (a swipe at lesbian love?) reflects a misanthropic and misogynistic consciousness where 'hack off his pendants' segues into the parody of Eliot's 'The awful daring of a moment's surrender/which an age of prudence can never retract.' Bunting glosses and subverts, hinting at further notions of deviancy: 'can a moment of madness make up for/an age of consent?' In the final section of the poem we have the reference to a soldier who 'Debauched the neighbor's little girl/to save two shillings...' (CP 44). The final stanza of Section Three, not without a growing hysteria, with its 'choking on onion skin' and 'slops of porridge', not only makes the pig's dinner into a prevailing metaphor, but it also recalls the guiles of Circe which both entrap and mollify the prisoner in *Villon*. Several plates are now spinning in the air. 'The Gadarene swihine have got us in tow' (CP 43) recalls the gospel account of the devils cast into swine and parodies the well-known contemporary song 'The Liverpool girls have got us in tow' (PBB 171). The echo of Circe reminds us of Ulysses' journey into the underworld.

Section Four opens with an epigraph from Canto 7 of the *Inferno* which takes the reader into the most powerful part of Bunting's poem.

> *Ed anche vo' che tu per certo credi*
> *che sotto l'acqua ha gente che sospira.*

(CP 44)

Bunting translates this towards the end of the piece – 'and besides I want you to know for certain/there are people under the water. They are sighing.' The beginning of Section Four takes us a little further ahead in Dante's account of the damned:

> Stuck in the mud they are saying: 'We were sad
> in the air, the sweet air the sun makes merry,
> we were glum of ourselves, without a reason;
> now we are stuck in the mud and therefore sad.'
> That's what they mean, but the words die in their throat;
> they cannot speak out because they are stuck in the mud.
> Stuck, stick, Styx. Styx, eternal, a dwelling.

(CP 44)

In Dante's fifth circle of hell the wrathful and the depressed are plunged beneath the waters of the Styx and, in the light of the emotional pitch of both *Attis* and *The Well*, there's an appropriateness in taking the reader into this section. The general climate of the poem is now illuminated by the specific sufferings of the damned. Bunting observes, writing to Makin towards the end of his life, 'In the Commedia, Medusa makes her appearance just after Dante has made acquaintance with the "accidiosi". Chaucer has the word, but it has vanished from modern English and all its very complex meaning is forgotten [...] It is essentially hopelessness, no longer a cardinal sin, perhaps because the industrial revolution has condemned so large a proportion of our population to wallow in it.' Bunting continues, now offering a critique of *Briggflatts*: 'You may reasonably conclude that it is a sin I feel myself much inclined to, to be cured or nullified by the epicurean slowworm rather than by Alexander's heroics' (*SV* 94–5).

Anger and melancholy in Canto 7 slip into dread and cowardice in Canto 8 which anticipates the Gorgon's ferocity of Canto 9; in effect the trajectory of Bunting's early sonatas overlaps with Cantos 7–9 from Dante's *Inferno*. Bunting argued: 'I am inescapably part of a detested generation. To see, and to have a mirror amongst what you see, is less than usual in satire. Hence the difficulty' (*PBB* 175). There's a certain amount of 'useful' self-loathing in all of this and that 'detested generation' has a Romantic frisson about it too. Yet Bunting's post-1918 lamentations are never entirely solipsistic. He also operates as a cultural critic, conscious of the possibilities and limits of poetic solutions in Auden's 'low dishonest decade'. In *Briggflatts*, 'It looks well on the page, but never/well enough' (*CP* 67); in Rudaki's poem 'the title-page of my book was Love and Poetry' (*CP* 155); in *The Well* 'this page/[is] ripped from Love's ledger and Poetry's' (*CP* 45). Such commentary, habitually meta-poetic, continues to interrogate the poet's own sense of artistic worth. The emotional charge of this somewhat raggedy sonata comes from its cultural-historical awareness. If 'the bones of a dead-man' in *Villon* hint at the slaughter of the 1914–18 war, the fourth section of *The Well* takes the reader directly back to the trenches:

> ulcers of mustard gas, a rivet in the lung
> from scrappy shrapnel,
> frostbite, trench-fever, shell-shock,
> self-inflicted wound,

tetanus, malaria, influenza.
Swapped your spare boots for a packet of gaspers.

(*CP* 44)

These lines recall the poetry of Wilfred Owen et al. Yet it's in this re-formulation of the Dantean narrative – the damned stuck in the mud, whispering ghosts in the fields of France – that Bunting most powerfully evokes the hellishness of trench warfare. *The Well of Lycopolis*, whose title has lupine associations, is not only in itself an example of war poetry after the event, but also has an uncannily prefiguring dimension. If Bunting was imprisoned for refusing to enlist for the First World War, he would some five years after the writing of this poem 'Join the Royal Air force/and see the World' (*CP* 44). In Owen's words 'The Poetry is in the pity'; in *The Well* Bunting nuances the infernal with a late lyrical charge. Deferred love and exquisite poetry are, at the last minute, glimpsed *in the mud*:

> The surface bubbled and boils with their sighs.
> Look where you will see it.
> The surface sparkles and dances with their sighs
> as though Styx were silvered by a wind from Heaven.

(*CP* 45)

AUS DEM ZWEITEN REICH

The allowance that Bunting received from Margaret de Silver in 1928 allowed him to 'clear [...] off to Germany' (D). Berlin would have been an understandable destination for a young poet. These were the years of the Weimar Republic and writers such as Auden and Isherwood later gravitated towards the German capital. Isherwood's writing, in particular, documented a modern, tolerant city that enjoyed a short-lived cultural renaissance before the Nazis took power in 1933. Bunting had already lived in London and Paris. His 'Berlin period' was, however, short-lived, not least because he 'didn't like the Germans at all' (D). In Bunting's portrait of Berlin, promiscuity becomes an analogue of sexual lack. 'Naked cabarets/in Jaegerstrasse' are an inverted image of Attis 'grieving for his testicles'. Both suggest some kind of psychological and/or spiritual dysfunction. Suter sees *Aus Zem Zweiten Reich* as a

53

'minor [...] and more lighthearted Waste Land. We see the sterility of a ruined society.'[40]

Bunting's *disprezzo* for Berlin is apparent in the opening stanza:

> Women swarm in Tauentsienstrasse.
> Clients of Nollendorferplatz cafes,
> shadows on sweaty glass,
> hum, drum on the table
>   to the negerband's faint jazz.

(CP 36)

'Swarm', 'shadows', even 'negerband', create another set of infernal urban images, yet the thrust of the poem's attack is directed against a brittle, materialistic modernity where the use of rhyme has a marshalling, even coercive effect. This is a city of

> efficiently whipped cream,
> efficiently metropolitan chatter and snap,
> transparent glistening wrapper
>   for a candy pack.

(CP 36)

The typist in *The Waste Land* who smoothes 'her hair with automatic hand' after meaningless sex in her bed-sit becomes a representative of the modern metropolis. In similar fashion, although here the German 'accent' is brought to the fore, Bunting suggests a robotic soullessness: 'automatic, somewhat too clean' becomes 'rapid, dogmatic, automatic and efficient,/ *ganz modern* (my italics, CP 36). The purchase on the contemporary is reinforced by a reference to Pudovkin's propagandist film *Sturm uber Asien* (1928). The ideological, and prophetic, implications of the film are not lost in a poem set in a German city never devoid of ideological charge. Yet the film is not being shown today; in its place there's some cheap titillation where 'The person on the screen,/divorced and twenty-five, must pass for fourteen.' She wears 'a widenecked shirt with nothing underneath/so that you can see her small breasts when she/often bends towards the camera' (CP 36). The audience, mostly male, we are told, 'stirs' and the narrator 'is teased too', preferring the public blonde to the brunette by his side. In this city of 'naked cabarets' their relationship is appropriately de-personalized, finding its romantic apotheosis in one of the poem's stilted utterances: 'If, smoothing this silk skirt, you pinch my thighs,/

that will be fabelhaft' (*CP* 37).

Both *Attis* and *The Well* convey a sense of European Weltschmerz and the crisis of modernity. In *Aus Dem Zweiten Reich*, Berlin becomes the reified modern metropolis, a concrete example of the modern *cauchemar*. One of the virtues of the poem is the way in which Bunting creates a distinct morphology of the city, forgoing a mythological dynamic in favour of a type of realism. Street names and iconic place names, including the Gedächtnis Kirche and the Bahnhof Zoo, map out the contours of the capital. Bunting creates a set of sharp vignettes. In the second section Herr Lignitz becomes our (Virgillian) guide. Pornography has become the art of choice in the Weimar Republic. Bunting's habitual use of direct speech creates an immediacy. Herr Lignitz's championing of Berlin sets up the poet's condemnation of it:

> You have no naked pictures in your English magazines.
> It is shocking. Berlin is very shocking to the English. Are you
>   shocked?
> Would you like to see the naked cabarets
> in Jaegerstrasse? I think there is
> nothing like that in Paris.
> Or a department store. They are said to be
> almost equal to Macy's in America.

>   (*CP* 37)

The third section of the poem, a poem that barely spills onto the third page, makes the German poet and playwright Gerhart Hauptmann the focus of Bunting's scornful attack (*PBB* 168). Hauptmann is never mentioned by name yet in his notes Bunting writes 'The great man need not be identified but will, I believe, be recognized by those who knew him' (*CP* 225). The young poet clearly felt some animus towards the Nobel prize winner and one imagines that the irritation may have been fostered in Rapallo where Hauptman came to winter as another 'grand old man of letters'. Writing the poem in Rapallo, Bunting attaches Hauptman to his Berlin sketches, in all likelihood drawing on Max Beerbohm's caricature of 'that windswept chevelure'. The self-regarding vanity of the ageing German clearly got under Bunting's skin. The suggestion here is that Hauptmann personifies lack of sincerity, lack of engagement and a preening self-importance:

Who talked about poetry,
and he said nothing at all;
plays,
and he said nothing at all;
politics,
and he stirred as if a flea
bit him.

(CP 38)

He becomes an emblem of reputation over substance and the gothicized *Schrecklich* describes not only Bunting's Berlin experience but feeds into the poet's wider analysis of contemporary culture. We should remember that the poems discussed in this chapter were largely composed in Fascist Italy. Bunting's sardonic scorn reaches a crescendo in the poem's ironic curtain call where all is obsequious glad-handing and charade. Bunting's contempt is palpable. 'Viennese bow from the hips', and project their 'contorted laudatory lips':

wreaths and bouquets surround
the mindless menopause.
Stillborn fecundities,
frostbound applause.

(CP 38)

The 'mindless menopause' bleeds into the oxymoron 'Stillborn fecundities'. Typically, Bunting denotes creative impasse with the trope of non-procreation. The equation has been tested variously in these early pieces and three decades later he will come back to it in the Kleinfeldt passage in *Briggflatts*. Here the un-consoled and unfulfilled poet-troubadour:

lies with one to long for another,
sick, self-maimed, self-hating,
obstinate, mating
beauty with squalor to beget lines still-born.

(CP 65)

4

Chomei at Toyama and *The Spoils*

Rather in the way that Bunting chanced upon Firdosi's *Shahnameh* on the quayside of Genoa, he had come across Marcello Muccioli's Italian translation of Kamo-no-Chomei's *Hōjōki*. Bunting's ten-page poem is a strategic redaction of the Italian's translation of twenty pages of thirteenth-century Japanese prose. The sonatas discussed in the last chapter reveal in various ways how the poet habitually moves between literary and linguistic cultures, weaving segments of the precursor texts into English, sometimes in a colloquial manner and sometimes creating an idiom which is intriguingly poised between the original language and a contemporary rendering. Villon and Dante loosen the chords of Bunting's poetic voice and now Chomei, via Muccioli's Italian prose, has a similarly facilitating effect. The act of translation is never reduced to some crimping philological exercise in verbal 'accuracy' which leaves behind a lifeless corpse; rather it seeks both distillation and the creation of an atmosphere out of which the new work emerges. The latter leans on the original but is not without its new-won independence. Suter argues, in fact, that *Chomei* 'stands entirely on its own. The reader need have no acquaintance with its source [...] which is entirely assimilated into both the design and subject matter.'[1] Bunting, like Pound, has an ear for cadence and was never short of intuition and what might be described as poetic instinct. There is, in Bunting's translations, an observable sympathy between poet and subject. Just as Bunting readily identifies with Villon, we can see how in *Chomei at Toyama* the English poet warms to that 'simpatico old Jap' (*PS* 62).

That 'simpatico old Jap' served at the court of the Emperor

Go-Toba. Bunting notes that Kamo-no-Chomei (1154–1216) 'belonged to the minor nobility of Japan and held various offices in the civil service. He applied for a fat job in a Shinto temple, was turned down, and next day announced his conversion to Buddhism [...] He retired from public life to a kind of mixture of hermitage and country cottage at Toyama on Mount Hino and there, when he was getting old, he wrote the Ho-Jo-Ki in prose, of which my poem is in the main a condensation' (CP 227). Chomei's renunciation of the world is considered a high point in the zuihitsu literary tradition (PBB 135). Basho claimed: 'Among diaries of the road, those of Ki, Chomei and the Nun Abutsu are consummate works, bringing to fulfilment the feelings of the journey, while later writers merely imitate their form, lapping their dregs, unable to create anything new.'[2] It is easy to see how Chomei's stoicism in the face of travail and flux coincides with a recognizable attitude emerging in Bunting's poems of the 1920s and 1930s. There is, however, a difference in tone. From Villon to The Well, Bunting often adopts the strategy of complaint which results most typically in an acerbic if cultured snarl. If the early Sonatas are not infrequently concerned with mutability and death, Chomei turns his back on office and cultivates wise acceptance:

> Hankering, vexation and apathy,
> that's the run of the world.
> Hankering, vexation and apathy,
> keeping a carriage wont cure it.
>
> (CP 93)

The Hōjōki is sometimes translated as 'An account of my Hut' or 'Life in a Dwelling Ten Feet Square' (PBB 134) and one can see how Chomei's quest for a mind-clearing simplicity was appealing to the sometimes truculent English poet. Chomei's abandonment of the material world and his Buddhist celebration of the higher life provided a model to a poet mired in the cultural politics of the metropolis. In fact, Chomei's embrace of solitude anticipates similar periods in Bunting's life. This quest for immanence serves as a good introduction to Briggflatts. Throughout much of Chomei it is not difficult to recognize a Weltanschauung that aligns itself to the 'philosophical' attitude of Bunting's magnum opus in which St Cuthbert is favoured over the egotistical heroics of Eric Bloodaxe. Monkish quietude, where Pound's exhortation 'Pull down thy vanity' echoes across the valley, not only describes the basic position of *Chomei*, it likewise anticipates the non-dogma of *Briggflatts*. Although Gary Synder's description of Bunting as a Buddhist was rejected by the English poet, one can trace from *Chomei* to *Briggflatts*, via some of the Persian translations, a broadly pantheistic attitude which draws on Buddhist/Quaker sensibilities and which is sympathetic to environmental issues.

Forde argues that the late Heian and early Kamakura Periods (1154–1216) parallel those in which Bunting was living: 'the military caste held power and the science of war was taking preference over intellectual matters' (*PBB* 134). Bunting was working on the poem only a handful of years before the outbreak of the Second World War and it seems plausible to suggest that Chomei's position of enlightened passivity corresponds at some level with Bunting's resolve as a conscientious objector in 1918. In various ways *Chomei* might be read as both an anti-war poem and even an anti-fascist poem. The routing of the *Hōjōki* through Muccioli, and now Bunting, a decade after Mussolini's march on Rome, creates an interesting set of reverberations. Chomei himself pens a historical document as well as a philosophical essay in the Confucian-Buddhist tradition and he was living during a period of considerable drama. The *Hōjōki* refers to the Great Fire that destroyed the capital Kyoto in 1177, the whirlwind or typhoon of 1180, the famine of 1181–2 and the earthquake of 1185. This narrative of catastrophes creates a verifiable backdrop against which Chomei adopts his position on mutability and impermanence. In the fifth stanza of Bunting's *Chomei* we find a set of questions remarkably similar to those asked in the coda of *Briggflatts*:

> Whence comes man at his birth? or where
> does death lead him? Whom do you mourn?

> (CP 85)

Bunting's *Chomei* leans on two texts: Muccioli's Italian translation (1930) and the original Japanese work by Kamo-no-Chomei (1212). Bunting had no Japanese and he was as dependent on Muccioli as Pound had been on Ernest Fenellosa when he was composing the *Cathay* poems. This cultural-linguistic mediation is a hallmark of the modernists' project and the poet encourages a form of creative slippage in the movement from text to text. Bunting tells us: 'I have taken advantage of Professor Muccioli's Italian version, together with his learned notes *to try to complete Chomei's work for him*' (my italics, CP 227). At moments, Muccioli's Italian notes inform Bunting's text as we see the English poet recreating 'the simpatico old Jap' in the poet's likeness even though Bunting later denied the poem's autobiographical element (*SV* 70). Prose translations of the *Hōjōki* are appropriately terse and translators tend to work at maintaining the elegant restraint of the original. There are two principal intervening operations in Bunting's *Chomei*. The twenty pages of prose, to begin with, are rendered into a ten page poem. This represents, in effect, a palpable example of the Pound/Bunting definition of poetry: Dichten = Condensare.[3] The *Hōjōki* begins:

> The flow of the river is ceaseless, and its water is never the same. The bubbles that float in the pools, now vanishing, now forming, are not of long duration: so in the world are man and his dwellings.[4]

Bunting responds:

> Swirl sleeping in the waterfall!
> On motionless pools scum appearing
> disappearing!

(CP 85)

If the reader places a prose translation of the *Hōjōki* next to Bunting's poetic reprise they see that the poetic version naturally quickens, sharpens and cuts. Much of the poem is driven by its laconic idiom ('I have been noting events for forty years' or 'men are fools to invest in real estate'). The movement from prose *into* poetry triggers a set of strategies regarding lineation and formal variation, involving longer, denser stanzas and pared-down utterance. The reduction of the text creates a pressure of its own where the distance between the documented disasters in the opening pages and the philosophizing of Chomei is foreshortened. The pressurizing dynamic of the shorter poetic text draws attention, not without its Bachelardian metaphysic, to the significance of dwelling. The account of 'The great earthquake of Genryaku' leads to 'This is the unstable world and/we in it unstable and our houses' (CP 88) and a little later Chomei prepares his exiguous abode that takes on the (not unhomely) qualities of a pre-death grave:

> The dew evaporates from my sixty years,
> I have built my last house, or hovel,
> a hunter's bivouac, an old
> silkworm's cocoon:
> ten feet by ten, seven high: and I,
> reckoning it a lodging not a dwelling,
> omitted the usual foundation ceremony.

(CP 89)

Yet, and this is significant, Bunting characteristically deflects solemnity by the interjection of a colloquial register. The hut on the hill is not without its conveniences:

> I have filled the frames with clay,
> set hinges at the corners;
> easy to take it down and carry it away
> when I get bored with this place.

(CP 89)

Chomei has rid himself from the conceit of possession:

> Two barrowloads of junk
> and the cost of a man to shove the barrow,
> no trouble at all.

(CP 90)

Bunting's *Chomei* employs various strategies: the presentation of 'concrete data' (SV 69), Pound's ideogrammic method, citation, apostrophe, lyrical interlude and ironic knowingness, where question mark, exclamation and use of italics become part of the armoury. Often the poem effects a pleasing exchange between a compressed (Haiku-like) meaningfulness and an attenuating levity, combining the colloquial with the urbane:

> I came here for a month
> five years ago.
> There's moss on the roof.
>
> And I hear Soanso's dead
> back in Kyoto.
> I have as much room as I need.

I know myself and mankind.

. . . . . .

I don't want to be bothered.

(CP 92)

Bunting's pared-down 'Japanese' style ensures the poem's sympathetic verve:

> Friends fancy a rich man's riches,
> friends suck up to a man in high office.
> If you keep straight you will have no friends
> but catgut and blossom in season.

(CP 92)

or

> I sweep my own floor
> – less fuss.
> I walk; I get tired
> but do not have to worry about a horse.

(CP 93)

It's difficult, in effect, not to be reminded of Pound's *Cathay* poems, deferred war poems in their own right. Eliot claimed that Pound 'invented Chinese poetry for our time' and Bunting seizes on the inadequacy of later translators in the 'Chinese-Fenollosa-Pound' school. They did not have 'Pound's skill to turn a pause in the rhythm into emotion, *nor his daring to supplement or alter the original to clinch the movement into a poem*'[5] (my italics). One might argue that Bunting's *Chomei* acts as a bridge between Pound's *Cathay* poems and the later work of Gary Snyder and Robert Hass, not to mention the Scottish poet Kenneth White. Avant-garde interest in Chinese and Japanese poetry has given rise to what White has called the 'Cold Mountain School'.[6]

Bunting's critique of Pound's approach to translation not only describes his own methodology but also nicely pinpoints the *modus operandi* of *Chomei* itself. Part of that process is the way in which Bunting has reined in 'oriental lushness' (*SV* 67), allowing a colloquial, modernizing idiom. Friends 'suck up to a man in high office' and 'Men are fools to invest in real estate' and havoc is inflicted on 'Sixth Avenue' and the city is 'flooded with gangsters' and hapless crowds resemble 'demobilized conscripts'.

62

Any possible sententiousness wrapped around Chomei's spiritual life is playfully undercut by Bunting's less reverential attitude. The poet explains in his notes: 'I cannot take his Buddhism solemnly considering the manner of his conversion [...] and his whole urbane, sceptical and ironical temper' (*CP* 227). In effect, Bunting ironicizes further, injecting a pleasing layer of mischief. This rescues the text from solemnity and actually succeeds in giving Chomei recognizable human characteristics which hint at the curmudgeonly as well as certain types of emotional disbelief. Bunting never idealizes Chomei. We find ourselves moving between 'One generation/I saddened myself with idealistic philosophies' to:

> A fine moonlit night,
> I sit at the window with a headful of old verses
>
> *Whenever a monkey howls there are tears on my cuff.*
>
> (*CP* 91)

A build-up of seriousness in the text, such as the iconic description of 'the view from the summit: sky bent over Kyoto', is immediately qualified by a deadpan observation: 'a very economical way of enjoying yourself' (*CP* 91). The pilgrimage to Ishiyama ends in a borrowed quotation from the poet Seminaru, where 'scuttle' and 'quite satisfactory' enforce and finesse the idiomatic texture of the language:

> *Somehow or other*
> *we scuttle through a lifetime*
> *Somehow or other*
> *neither palace nor straw-hut*
> *is quite satisfactory.*
>
> (*CP* 91)

Makin argues that Bunting's Chomei *plays* more (*SV* 71); the hermit's solitary pleasures reveal appetite *and* imperfection:

> Be limber, my fingers, I am going to play *Autumn Wind*
> to the pines, I am going to play *Hastening Brook*
> to the water. I am no player
> but there's nobody listening,
> I do it for my own amusement.
>
> (*CP* 91)

By the end of the poem we feel that Chomei's position hasn't led to euphoric enlightenment, but a kind of grudging acceptance. 'I am out of place in the capital', he says 'people take me for a beggar'; but he turns this round and argues 'You are so – I regret it – welded to your vulgarity' (*CP* 93). The last three stanzas, wonderfully modulated and free of melodrama, point to a state of affairs that suggests pragmatic accommodation and a useful lack of self-deception. Earlier, Chomei has described himself as 'a shifting rivermist, not to be trusted' (*CP* 93) and someone who doesn't ask 'anything extraordinary' of himself. Ultimately, Chomei is neither St Francis nor St Cuthbert but rather a Buddhist monk by force of circumstance and a certain inclination. He exhibits a pleasing lack of evangelical zeal and though, as he tells us, he is a man of 'passionate nature' he has, through his solitariness and enforced simplicity, found a poetic way of dealing with the world. He has done this without falling prey to the irrationality of the priestly followers of Cybele. Chomei's saintliness, one might argue, is Quaker-like in its practical modesty:

> Oh! There's nothing to complain about.
> Buddha says: 'None of the world is good.'
> I am fond of my hut...
>
> I have renounced the world;
> have a saintly
> appearance.
>
> I do not enjoy being poor,
> I've a passionate nature.
> My tongue
> clacked a few prayers.

> (*CP* 94)

THE SPOILS

There's a hiatus of some fifteen years between the writing of *The Well* and *The Spoils* (1951). This didn't preclude the composition of a handful of Odes (*CP* 126–32) and several translations or 'Overdrafts', to use Bunting's term (*CP* 155–60). In fact, his engagement with Rudaki, Manuchehri and Sa'di makes its way into the writing of *The Spoils*. Bunting's cultural range had been far-reaching: Villon's fifteenth-century Paris, various narratives from classical mythology, the early medieval period of the Japanese Emperor Go-Toba. Here, in *The Spoils*, Bunting positions the reader in a decisively Middle Eastern context. Yet these pieces are never merely historical vignettes. The past illuminates the present, and *vice versa*.

Bunting wrote *The Spoils* in Italy after the Second World War. Although the poem is never autobiographical in a revelatory sense, his knowledge of Persia informs the poem. *The Spoils* shows, as will *Briggflatts*, how bookish erudition and empirical engagement are welded closely together. Bunting's Middle-Eastern experiences took him directly into the campaigns of the Second World War: '*The Spoils* would be more of a public poem and less of a private phantasmagoria' (*SV* 101). The war years and their aftermath saw the transformation of Bunting from embattled poet into effective protagonist – aircraftsman, interpreter, spy, squadron leader, diplomat and *Times* journalist. He becomes, in effect, both a man of action and a cultural broker. These years gave him the opportunity to convert his enthusiasm for Firdosi's *Shahnameh* into a wider embrace of Middle Eastern culture. Makin argues: 'Persia confirmed and extended all the developments of his thinking. It was a particular kind of Paradise' (*SV* 103). He refers to a letter from Bunting to Dorothy Pound which describes Isfahan as a 'city so full of gardens and orchards that from a mile or two away you see only a forest with a few domes and minarets sticking up from it' (*SV* 103). We are reminded that Pound would have read these letters from within 'the institutionalized babble of a public mental hospital'. There, from *books*, he endeavoured to create in the *Cantos* 'the high-mountain ice and emerald world of the western China that Joseph Rock had known'. Makin imagines that 'It must have cut his heart to read what Bunting had been living' (*SV* 103).

Death as well as death-in-life stalk Bunting's early work. Theories about impermanence are now converted into accounts of warfare, where death and the possibility of death are common currency. *The Spoils* can be read as a Second World War poem and a meditation on war in general. Bunting is not traditionally seen as a 'soldier-poet' yet there is some overlap with the writings of Keith Douglas whose brief literary career was cut short in 1944. Douglas was a tank commander in the North

African campaign and played an active role in the battle of El Alamein. Douglas' poetry is remarkable for its vivid and unsentimental detail. In the last stanza of 'Cairo Jag', we read:

> But by a day's travelling you reach a new world
> the vegetation is of iron
> dead tanks, gun barrels split like celery
> the metal brambles have no flowers or berries
> and there are all sorts of manure, you can imagine
> the dead themselves, their boots, clothes and possessions
> clinging to the ground, man with no head
> has a packet of chocolate and a souvenir of Tripoli.

The title of Bunting's poem, in fact, suggests 'The Spoils of War'. Yet the poem comes with two epigraphs, the first in Arabic, which is explained in the notes: – 'al anfal li'llah is from the Qor'an' and means 'The spoils are for God' (CP 225). By the end of the poem *spoils* has become a cognate of *ruins* and bleeds into the gerund *spoiling*, as the writing sets up a juxtaposition between a spiritual attitude that accommodates death as part of life and an oppositional materialism mired in commerce and soul-shrinking bureaucracy, a type of 'anti-life'. Cox sees 'the dominant theme' of the poem as a clash 'between the calculating and the reckless', thus establishing a 'bourgeois-romantic dichotomy'.[7] This sets up an argument around the 'differing attitudes toward life and death in Eastern and Western societies' (PBB 177–8). This is not to do with celebrating Islam in any theological sense but rather an opportunity for Bunting to express his delight in the manifestations of Islamic/Persian culture – poetry, music and architecture. For Pound, the China of Confucius represented a special kind of spiritual geography. Bunting found what he was looking for in Persia, a particular version of Epicureanism, and one might choose to read *The Spoils* as an argument against western colonial practice. The awareness of death has a quickening effect which enhances the virtues of pleasure. 'Condole with me with abundance of secret pleasure', we read in Section Three (CP 57), where we are now far removed from Dante's circle of hell reserved for the angry and spiritually depressed. Bunting's sympathies for Persia led him to argue that 'sooner or later we must absorb Islam if our culture is not to die of anaemia.'[8] Manifestations of Islamic culture in *The Spoils* are not without their textual complications and various

66

demands are made upon the reader which are not eased by Bunting's parsimonious notes. The poem is sometimes crowded with philosophers, poets, musicians, architects and Seljuk leaders.

Yet *The Spoils* is a poem, not an essay, and it is the nature of a sonata to set up a dialectic which reveals itself in a mosaic of interrelationships. Bunting's poems often work by conflation, the holding together of oppositional and appositional forces, and we have seen this in the poems so far discussed. Nevertheless, the poem's argument, from the outset, is clear enough:

> Man's life so little worth,
> do we fear to take or lose it?
> No ill companion on a journey, Death
> lays his purse on the table and opens the wine.
>
> (CP 47)

Not only is this a recapitulation of earlier poetic concerns, but it also anticipates the metaphysical dimension of *Briggflatts*. Here the personification of Death buying his wares in a tavern foregrounds the money nexus that runs through Section One and beyond. In the second stanza of Section Three the repeated reference to 'Lydian pebbles' recalls the Lydians whose king (Croesus) is said to have introduced gold and silver coin for the purpose of economic transaction. The presence of death, almost *simpatico* in this opening description, has a particular resonance in a poem about war. Although *The Spoils* has a discursive quality in its treatment of history and art, its most evocative sections are those which come out of the poet's experiences. Asshur, the first speaker in Section One, leaves the business of 'marking the register' and 'weighing coin' and provides an account of a military encampment which is historical, contemporary and compellingly vivid:

> Camels raise their necks from the ground,
> cooks scour kettles, soldiers oil their arms,
> snow lights up high over the north,
> yellow spreads in the desert, driving blue westward
> among banks, surrounding patches of blue,
> advancing in enemy land.
> Kettles flash, bread is eaten,

scarabs are scurrying rolling dung.
Thirty gorged vultures on an ass's carcass
jostle, stumble, flop aside, drunk with flesh,
too heavy to fly, wings deep with inner gloss.

(CP 47–8)

In Section Three, we return to the specifics of warfare and the context is largely contemporary. The fifth stanza cuts to 'Flight-lieutenant Idema' who 'wouldn't fight for Roosevelt' but dons a uniform for Churchill 'for fun of fighting and pride' who's subsequently 'lost/in best blues and his third plane that day' (CP 56). Idema's insouciance and sacrifice recall the opening stanza of the poem ('No ill companion on a journey, Death/lays his purse on the table and opens the wine') and displays an attitude that ties in with what Bunting sees as typifying an 'eastern' view, a coalescing of selflessness and fatalism. Bunting, a conscientious objector in the First World War, is now close to elevating the soldier-warrior into a romantic figure: 'O soldier! Hard muscles, nipples like spikes' (CP 49). Idema is becoming the transcendent outsider. It is interesting to ponder on correspondence sent to Zukofsky where, according to Bunting, war generates 'pleasures of its own' in which 'death is neither a bugbear, nor a consummation, but just happens' and is 'part of the fun' and 'that freedom from war [...] can be pursued at the expense of things better worth preserving than peace and plenty, of which, I should say, the most important , and the most threatened, is personal autonomy, Free will entails sin! I don't want my acts determined by any authority whatever' (PBB 201).

The poet gives us, as The Spoils nears its conclusion, an evocative description of the detritus of war which might recall the earlier passage by Douglas:

Broken booty, but usable
along the littoral, frittering into the south.
We marvelled, careful of craters and minefields,
noting a new-painted recognisance
on a fragment of fuselage, sand drifting into dumps,
a tank's turret twisted skyward,
here and there a lorry unharmed
out of fuel or the crew scattered;
leaguered in lines numbered for enemy units,
gulped beer of their brewing,

mocked them marching unguarded to our rear;
discerned nothing indigenous, never a dwelling,
but on the shore sponges stranded and beyond the reef
unstayed masts staggering in the swell,
till we reached readymade villages clamped on cornland,
empty, Arabs feeding vines to goats;
at last orchards aligned, girls hawked by their mothers
from tent to tent, Tripoli dark
under a cone of tracers.

(CP 56)

'Nothing indigenous' reminds us that the fighting recorded here
is a western conflict, taking place in an ancient terrain layered
like a palimpsest. The account above is followed by a reference
to the Carthaginian and Roman city of Leptis, now famed for its
ruins, and the site of earlier conflicts; the description of the
Arabs feeding vines to goats and the hawking of their daughters
takes us back to Section One with its narratives of transaction
and exchange. In the final passage of Section Three, Bunting
globalizes the motif of conflict – world war no less – by drawing
on personal experience. There are references to the hazards of
seamanship, air attacks ('Glasgow burning'), Baltic convoys
where the 'unintelligible sea' and 'the dear unintelligible ocean'
(CP 57) recall 'The sea has no renewal, no forgetting' (*Villon*, CP
29). Nor is it fanciful to suggest in the maelstrom of the air raid
that we get a glimpse of Eliot's 'dove descending' which 'breaks
the air/with flame of incandescent terror' (*Four Quartets*, 1942).
We are taken to Staithes, Yorkshire, where old men 'toil in the
bilge to open a link', where *link*, a keyword in *Briggflatts*, points
to the switch-back dynamics of a non-linear narrative, and
where 'a drowned Finn' and 'a drowned Chinee' (CP 57) recall
from Section One the flooded Tigris with its 'Dead camels, dead
Kurds' (CP 48). The poem seeks resolution through echoes and
symmetries both sustained and broken. In the 'Little Gidding'
section of *Four Quartets*, the poem's narrator meets Dante in the
bombed streets of London evoking an Inferno of another kind in
the burning metropolis. Although we are told that 'History is
now and England', Eliot's poem works largely through abstrac-
tions. Bunting is at his most successful when he holds onto
detail and, by recording events at the end of the poem, he sets
up his own binaries of fire and water, heat and cold:

From Largo Law look down,
moon and dry weather, look down
on convoy marshalled, filing between mines.
Cold northern, clear sea-gardens
between Lofoten and Spitzbergen,
as good a grave as any, earth or water.
What else do we live for and take part,
we who would share the spoils?

(CP 58)

If conflict, economic as well as military, runs like a backbone through the poem, *The Spoils* offers up a wider agenda. The poem's second epigraph, which refers to the sons of Shem, allows Bunting a wider lens in his appraisal of the Semitic peoples and enables him to draw on the Old Testament, a familiar text for a poet schooled in the Quaker tradition. Bunting's engagement with Persian poetry, not least its intricate patterning, acts upon *The Spoils* and this is particularly noticeable in Section One. Literary knowledge strengthens Bunting's understanding of the Middle East, making *The Spoils* a cultural paradigm in which materialism and colonialism are implicitly critiqued. The realist mode we observe elsewhere gives way to a more allusive manner and, in Section Two, we are given a rapid account of Persian history. After the question posed at the beginning of the poem – 'man's life so little worth/do we fear to take or lose it?' – we are introduced to four characters who represent a distinct yet colliding set of attitudes: Asshur the merchant-soldier, Lud (Lot, Sodom) the city dweller, Arpachshad, an ancestor of the desert tribes and Aram the exiled Jew. Bunting describes them as the adventurer, the Baghdadi, the Bedoin and 'the better modern Jewish mind' (*PBB* 179). Each character speaks three times, establishing a mosaic of voices, where Asshur's monologues are marked by bronze and pence, Lud's by coral, jet and jade, Arpachshad's by gold, silver, sand and moon and Aram's by vineyard and seed. The drive of the writing reveals a scorn for grubby economic imperatives and seeks, in its place, to celebrate a liberating sensuality: 'Thighs in a sunshaft, uncontrollable smile' (*CP* 49). The relationship between repressive economics and the development – or lack – of the creative-sexual self is explored in a number of ways. Asshur says:

> We bear witness against the merchants of Babylon
> that they have planted ink and reaped figures.

(CP 49)

And Lud speaks 'Against the princes of Babylon, that they have tithed of the best/leaving sterile ram, weakly hogg to the flock' (*CP* 49), whilst Arpachshad indicts commercial activity with a disparaging list of city occupations: 'tailors, hairdressers, jewellers, perfumers' (*CP* 49). Babylon is *the* tainted metropolis and Arpachshad probably reminds Bunting of the Bakhtiari tribesmen. Aram's final response speaks to the opening stanza. The life-as-journey motif, where Death is our wine-opening companion, is nuanced in the clatter of coin and spilt wine:

> What's begotten on a journey but souvenirs?
> Life we give and take, pence in a market,
> without noting beggar, dealer, changer;
> pence we drop in the sawdust with spilt wine.

(CP 50)

Sections Two and Three are not without their *longeurs*. The original plan was to create a four-part poem but in the quest for a greater economy Bunting spliced and over-conflated and was aware of creating a certain 'lopsidedness'. Bunting the Persian expert, journalist and diplomat gets in the way of Bunting the poet (*SV* 117). At times the relationship between 'showing' and 'telling' is inadequately weighted. We are reminded of those moments in Pound's *Cantos* where 'luminous detail' is assumed rather than achieved. Bunting ultimately resolves the problem of structure in *Briggflatts*. The trajectory of thought, however, is clear enough. The opening of Section Two takes the reader into the flourishing period of the Turkish Seljuks who ruled over Persia in the eleventh and twelfth centuries. We are given a description of the Masjid-e Jom'a mosque, a fine example of early Persian architecture, built in Isfahan in the eleventh century during the reign of Malek Shah. The construction of the 'domes and avians' (or arches) anticipates later gothic edifices and discloses the mathematical sophistication of Islamic culture. Omar Khyyám, whom we tend to think of as the author of the *Rubáiyát*, is referred to in his guise as mathematician-philosopher and believer in metempsychosis. Equally significant is the reference to Avicenna, the Islamic philosopher-scientist noted

71

for reintroducing Aristotelian philosophy into the western tradition. The superiority of the Islamic Golden Age is implied in the reference to La Giralda, a construction in Seville which although built with Islamic design was executed with inferior craftsmanship. If both Sections One and Three inscribe the notion of the ephemeral, Bunting now draws the reader's attention to the possibility of artistic permanence.

The poetry of architecture is converted into poetry itself to create a clinching moment. Architecture as 'frozen music' becomes music itself. Bunting's memories take us to the lyrical heart of the city:

> Flute,
> shade dimples under chenars
> breath of Naystani chases and traces
> as a pair of gods might dodge and tag between stars.

(CP 52)

And after music comes a beautiful evocation of *life as art* where human activity and the natural word enact a poetic congruity. These two stanzas juxtapose cultural manifestation with pettifogging bureaucracy:

> A fowler spreading his net
> over the barley, calls,
> calls on a rubber reed.
> Grain nods in reply.
> Poppies blue upon white
> wake to the sun's frown.
> Scut of gazelle dances and bounces
> out of the afternoon.
> Owl and wolf to the night.
> On a terrace over a pool
> vafur, vodka, tea,
> resonant verse spilled
> from Onsori, Sa'di,
> till the girls' mutter is lost
> in whisper of stream and leaf,
> a final nightingale
> under a fading sky
> azan on their quiet.
>
> They despise police work,
> are not masters of filing:

> always a task for foreigners
> to make them unhappy,
> unproductive and rich.

(CP 53)

Section Two ends with a carefully observed *and* symbolic falcon. Not only was 'falcon' the name of Toghril, the first Seljuk conqueror, the predatory bird recalls and redeems the vultures gorging on 'an ass's carcass' in Section One (*CP* 47). Here the falcon 'unforseen/and absolute' has evaded the fowler's net and takes on the avenging quality of a higher power.[9] Once again it drags Eliot's descending dove with its 'flame of incandescent terror' from our poetic consciousness and evokes something of the drama of aerial bombings depicted in Tullio Crali's Futurist aeropainting 'Nose-Diving on the City' (1939). The falcon is Death's lordly representative, taking us back to the beginning of the poem.

> Have you seen a falcon stoop
> accurate, unforeseen
> and absolute, between
> wind-ripples over harvest? Dread
> of what's to be, is and has been –
> were we not better dead?

(CP 53)

5

Odes and Overdrafts

Personal Column
…As to my heart, that may as well be forgotten
or labelled: Owner will dispose of same
to a good home, refs. exchgd., h.&c.,
previous experience desired but not essential
or let on a short lease to suit convenience.

(CP 102)

Ode number 6 from the *First Book of Odes* was written in 1927. The manner of its delivery is of particular interest. The rancher twirls his rope before lassoing the target. The title, which draws us to a lonely-hearts column, flags up the modernity of the piece and the writing is a good example of Bunting's colloquial manner. Notwithstanding its knockabout and self-deprecating brio there's candour in its declaration. We have seen examples of the poet's allusive poetic and this approach needs to be put alongside Bunting's more direct way of writing. From the early poems onwards we can see how the poet employs an opaque, recondite manner but can also push through with a sharper line of attack, sometimes creating a poetry of statement. The juxtaposition of Bunting's 'literary' voice and his more 'personal' voice can be traced from the early work in the 1920s up until Ode 12 (CP 146) from the *Second Book of Odes*, which he wrote towards the end of his life. Ode 6 – or *'Personal Column'* – would appear to come from the school of hard knocks, yet the transaction between recorded experience and literary creation is necessarily complicated. The short piece also enjoys a 'buttoned-up' quality, adhering to the modernist notion of impersonality, yet it also bears the wounds of experience; 'you can't write about anything unless you've experienced it; you're either confused in your subject matter or else you get it all wrong' (*PBB* 107).

The vulnerability of the heart is a traditional poetic subject and the odes, from both the *First Book* (1924–49) and the *Second Book* (1964–80), confirm that Bunting was a poet of lyrical gifts. The poet describes his odes as sonnets to be sung and it is worth noting the form's choral tradition. Derived from the Greek word *aoiden*, the ode was 'originally a poem intended or adapted to be sung to instrumental accompaniment' (*PBB* 83). Literary historians make a distinction between the Pindaric and the Horatian ode and one of the early and most successful English practitioners was Edmund Spenser. Bunting employs the ode in an irregular and generic manner, sometimes creating forms of address, or apostrophe, as well as pieces weighted with satirical bite. The ode has an impressive literary pedigree and it provided Bunting with an array of poetic strategies: alliteration, assonance, onomatopoeia, rhyme and slant rhyme as well as tonal variation. Forde points out that 'some seem to have been written as technical exercises in which Pound, Zukofsky and others were involved', and although she argues that 'many are stepping stones thematically and technically to later, more mature work' (*PBB* 84), the brevity of the form allows Bunting a particularly direct purchase which results in some impressive *exempla*. The ode in the hands of Bunting, stepping free from the complex orchestrations of sonata form, sometimes enjoys a nakedly emphatic quality.

The collected and uncollected odes span his writing career from 1924 to 1980 and constitute a significant component of his oeuvre. Several of the earlier odes appeared in *Redimiculum Matellarum* (1930) and several of these pieces touch on themes which are taken up in *Briggflatts*. There's an interesting range too. It's worth noting Ode 17 (*CP* 113), dedicated to Mina Loy, which provides the trace of a submerged *British* modernist tradition. Ode 20, entitled 'Vestiges' (*CP* 116), employs the exquisite 'oriental' poetic we observed in *Chomei at Toyama*, whereas Ode 37, 'On the Fly-Leaf of Pound's Cantos' (*CP* 132), is not only a form of debt repayment, it also effects a succinct critique of Pound's work. Of the unpublished odes the most affecting is the poem dedicated to his son entitled 'A Song for Rustam' (*CP* 197).

The relationship between the two books is of interest. Poems from the *First Book* often dwell on the creative process itself, creating a meta-poetic dynamic also observed in the early Sonatas. If, frequently, the pieces have romantic, mortality and societal concerns, they are at their most revelatory when they're quarrying ideas of inspiration and process. They create a conversation about the risks and dilemmas *of choosing the métier of poetry*, and how to keep writing poetry when the muse, not infrequently in the guise of Polymnia, see Ode 5 (*CP* 101), withholds as well as provides. The 'Poet appointed' dare 'not decline/to walk among the bogus' (*CP* 65). In the *Second Book* we find 'What the Chairman Told Tom', a *jeu d'esprit* with a sting in its tail (*CP* 140). The Tom in question is Tom Pickard. The youthful poet is treated with contempt by the self-righteous Chairman, a recognizable representative of the commercial world:

> Poetry? It's a hobby.
> I run model trains.
> Mr Shaw there breeds pigeons.
>
> It's not work. You dont sweat.
> Nobody pays for it.
> You *could* advertise soap.

If George Orwell compared advertising to 'the rattling of a stick inside a swill bucket', the uncleanliness of poetry is taken up by the vexed Chairman:

> Nasty little words, nasty long words,
> it's unhealthy.
> I want to wash when I meet a poet.

> (*CP* 140)

Bunting admitted a susceptibility to the condition of *accidie* and we have seen in both *Attis* and *The Well* how Dantean notions of 'cowardice' are recruited to describe the creative anguish of the self-damning poet (*SV* 94). Medieval accounts of *accidie*, which might be described as 'sloth' or, in today's language, depression, revealed special dangers for the religious orders, yet mystics such as John of the Cross and Theresa of Avila considered the spiritual aridity of *accidie* as 'almost a precondition for a life of eternal bliss'[1]. By the time of the Renaissance the connection between melancholy and creativity had been forged and Bunting might be seen as post-Renaissance Epicurean, or a misanthropic sensualist – 'Sniff the sweet narcotic distilled by coupled/skins' (*CP* 105) – whose Muse is tantalizingly inconstant. The relationship between creative joy and sexual euphoria creates its own metaphor. The dry heart seeks liberation in the creative/procreative moment and the matrix of doubt and fulfilment finds its apogee in *Briggflatts*' lyrical high notes. The relationship between the *First Book* and the *Second Book* reveals a paradox. If the anxiety of stalled inspiration furnishes many of the earlier pieces, that anxiety is borne out in Bunting's creative paralysis between the early 1950s and the mid-1960s. The return of poetic inspiration in the 1960s sees the poet in his 'September Years'. Polymnia presents herself to a poet rather longer in the tooth, or allowing ourselves to skip back to Bunting's translation of Rudaki, *losing his teeth* (*CP* 155).

Ode 1, dated 1924, might seem little more than the striking of a poetic attitude. Originally entitled 'Sad Spring', it's tempting to read the poem as a response to the opening of *The Waste Land* yet it also anticipates the 'fear of spring' in the first section of *Briggflatts*. The transformation of spring from season of anticipation into unexpected menace, where April is now 'the cruellest month', might have its modernist origins in Stravinsky's *Rite of Spring* (1913).[2] Bunting gives us:

> Weeping oaks grieve, chestnuts raise
> mournful candles. Sad is spring
> to perpetuate, sad to trace
> immortalities never changing.

> (*CP* 97)

By the time he is writing Ode 3 a couple of years later (*CP* 99), Bunting has achieved something of that heightened poetic that becomes part of his armoury and which can be juxtaposed with his more demotic, satirical pieces. See, for example, the withering contempt shown in 'The Passport Officer' (*CP* 119). Ode 3, originally called 'Foam', is dedicated to Peggy Mullet and joins that group of poems which draws attention to the addressee. The poem was, in fact, a favourite of Yeats. It begins:

> I am agog for foam. Tumultuous come
> with teeming sweetness to the bitter shore

>   tidelong unrinsed and midday parched and numb
>   with expectation.

(CP 99)

Measuring the ebb and flow of the rhythmic tide, the poem becomes a whipped-up version of Matthew Arnold's 'Dover Beach'. The give and take of the sea-charge becomes a trope for the creative and sexual act as well as its subsequent loss.

>   Its indifference
>   haunts us to suicide. Strong memories
>   of sprayblown days exasperate impatience
>   to brief rebellion and emphasise
>   the casual impotence we sicken of.

'Mad waves', now 'braceletted with foam', rekindle the 'exuberance of unexplained desire' until the gods ordain:

>   renewed inevitable hopeless calm
>   and the foam dies and we again subside
>   into our catalepsy, dreaming foam,
>   while the dry shore awaits another tide.

(CP 99)

Catalepsy/ecstasy are the parameters of Bunting's creative template and the high-wiredness of that combination is re-examined in 'Chorus of Furies' (CP 106) which anticipates the Dantean interventions in Attis and The Well. There's an almost Elizabethan fever in this fear of creative loss:

>   He will lapse into a halflife lest the taut force
>   of the mind's eagerness
>   recall those fiends or new apparitions endorse
>   his excessive distress.

The metaphor of castration, or self-castration, stands for Bunting's oedipal-psychological Armageddon where the poet risks either the ill-judged passions of Attis or the contempt of the philistine capitalist as in 'What the Chairman Told Tom'. Non-creation is a kind of annihilation but the poetic act itself is never free of risk in a 'society hostile to the poet'.[3] Bunting is particularly adept at taking the reader into these alienating realms where inspiration and composition are subject to complex negotiation:

78

He will shrink, his manhood leave him, slough selfaware
the last skin of the flayed: despair.
He will nurse his terror carefully, uncertain
even of death's solace,
impotent to outpace
dispersion of the soul, disruption of the brain.

(CP 106)

If the return of the muse is heralded in the first ode of the *Second Book* – 'A thrush in the syringa sings' (*CP* 135) – the rattle of time's wingèd chariot qualifies any unconstrained delight. 'Death thrusts hard' and from 'a shaken bush' the poet lists 'familiar things/fear, hunger, lust'. The closing apostrophe – 'O gay thrush!' – attends ironically to these darker notes. At the moment of Bunting's resurrection we find the poet writing 'You idiot! What makes you think decay will/never stink from your skin?' There's an interesting relationship between Ode 4 (*CP* 138) and the earlier translation from Rudaki, briefly mentioned above. The drama of *tempus fugit* which runs from *Villon* through to *Briggflatts*, and which is all-apparent in Ode 4, is important in this Persian poem. The aged speaker draws attention to his physical decrepitude: 'All the teeth ever I had are worn down and fallen out.' Bodily decay becomes not only its own form of *memento mori* but a prompt for a philosophical enquiry into mutability and transformation on a wider scale: 'Many a broken desert has been gay garden,/many gay gardens grow where there used to be desert' (*CP* 155). Yet Rudaki, who speaks in his own name as he addresses a young woman, assumes the role of the 'gerontian' poet who makes his decline into a philosophy of regret:

What can you know, my blackhaired beauty,
what I was like in the old days?
You tickle your lover with your curls
but never knew the time when he had curls.

The poem continues:

The days are past when bold men sought his company,
the days are past when he managed affairs of princes,
the days are past when all wrote down his verses,
the days are past when he was the Poet of Khorassan.

(CP 156)

Ode 4 re-produces Villon's yearning lament: 'Where are the snows of yesteryear?' In effect, Bunting's translation of Rudaki (1948) would seem to collide with the later ode and in both cases the theatricality of advancing age mocks the past:

> You idiot! What makes you think decay will
> never stink from your skin? Your warts sicken
> typists, girls in the tube avoid you. Must they
> also stop their ears to your tomcat
> wailing, a promise your body cannot keep?

> (CP 138)

The aging poet continues to assume the role of sexual conquistador yet the heroic script is belied by performance:

> A lame stag, limping after the hinds, with tines
> shivered by impact and scarred neck – but
> look! Spittle fills his mouth, overflows,
> snuffing their sweet scent. His feet lift lightly
> with mere memory of gentler seasons.

> (CP 138)

The poem pulls out of autobiographical mode by taking us to the narrative of the aged (impotent) David who, shivering with the cold, is sent a beautiful virgin – Abishag the Shunammite – to keep him warm:

> Did the girl shrink from David? Did she hug his
> ribs, death shaking them, and milk dry
> the slack teat from which Judah had sucked life?

> (CP 138)

Odes 9–12 from the *Second Book* (CP 143–6) are of special interest. They are post-*Briggflatts* pieces and have their own crepuscular sensibility. Ode 11, '*At Briggflatts meetinghouse*', takes us back to the site of the great poem itself. A 'delight in transience' underscores the ephemeral and 'Boasts time mocks cumber Rome' acknowledges the meditative simplicity at the heart of the Quaker tradition. Bunting's last published ode (CP 146) evokes Eliot's 'Ash Wednesday':

> Because I do not hope to turn again
> Because I do not hope
> Because I do not hope to turn.

80

Like Eliot, Bunting draws on Cavalcanti's ballad 'Perch'i' no Spero di Tornar Mai Giammai'.[4] His first line adapts the Italian before resorting to signature imagery:

> Now we've no hope of going back,
> cutter, to that grey quay
> where we moored twice and twice unwillingly
> cast off our cables to put out at the slack
> when the sea's laugh was choked to a mutter.

> (CP 146)

Ode 12 enacts the sailor-poet's plangent valediction.[5] Bunting is unflinching in his consideration of last things. The boat is heaved free of the sands to become a type of floating coffin, a kind of ship burial. 'On naked banks a few birds strut' and the half moon, we are told, will do as it pleases. Echoing the coda from *Briggflatts*, Bunting signs out with 'We have no course to set,/only to drift too long, watch too glumly, and wait,/wait'(CP 146).

OVERDRAFTS

> 'Those who seek fortune afar find it the first.'

> (CP 157)

Bunting chose to call his translations Overdrafts which suggests from the outset that the poet was implicitly taking up a position in the complex discussion regarding the translatability of poetry. Nowadays that discussion invariably begins with Robert Frost's argument that poetry is lost in translation. He believed that 'there should always be a lingering unhappiness in reading translations.' This guarded view, and this from the poet who cited the old proverb 'Good fences make good neighbors' in his poem 'Mending Wall', would seem to resonate with Philip Larkin's provincial gestures: 'A writer can only have one language, if that language is going to mean anything to him.'[6] Both poets resisted the international dimension of modernism, generally rooting for home-grown poetic virtues, whether American or English. 'Good fences make good neighbours' came to describe post-1945 ideological divisions. During the Cold War, translation had the air of a diplomatic mission. For the modernists, however,

81

translation was the *sine qua non* of poetic activity as well as a way of learning one's craft. Donald Davie reminds us that the models which enabled Eliot at the beginning of his career 'were just not available in English but only in French'.[7] To *translate* is to cross national and cultural boundaries and the modernist generation was not short of émigrés. *Dépaysement* nourished creativity, and living outside one's own linguistic culture made translation an entirely congruous, even necessary practice. Whilst Larkin argued 'I believe that every poem must be its own sole freshly created universe', modernist poetry subscribed to the belief that poems were haunted by other poems whatever their linguistic provenance.

Later conversations regarding translation strategy often coalesce around the differing positions of Robert Lowell and Vladimir Nabokov. Lowell's *Imitations* (1961) heralds a creative promiscuity whilst Nabokov insists on the notion of fidelity. Davie, who rejects the rigidity of Frost, alights on a position that appears to be a combination of pragmatism and serendipity. Well-disposed towards the poetry of Pound and Bunting, he maintains that the translation of poetry is 'a noble office' if 'damnably difficult' and that ultimately 'Poetry *is* translatable – just, sometimes, given luck given above all a scrupulous and gifted and lucky (which is to say, inspired) translator.'[8] This position serves as an introduction to Bunting's Overdrafts. The word itself implies a modesty of sorts as well as a belief in the inter-dependence of poetry whilst eschewing an overly theoretical stance; it has an appropriately workmanlike quality about it as well as suggesting the poet's sense of indebtedness. And indebtedness has a particular resonance for a poet 'accustomed to penury'. To take out an overdraft 'is usually to smoothen cash flow problems; in this case by translating these works, the poet keeps his own poetry moving, in currency, in credit'.[9] These transactions, for Bunting, were a combination of method, stimulus and possibility and Cid Corman is right to argue that translation was central to Bunting's achievement. He points out that 'There is a sense both of Horace – classical music – and Arabic (Persian) lyricism running over and under and through the entire oeuvre', hence Bunting's work in general is informed by the *habit* of translation. Corman is alert to the musicality of Bunting's poetry, and poetic borrowings helped with this: 'it is impossible to read Bunting's work [...] without wanting to "say" the words – to get the weight and substance and sense of them on the tongue – via breath and mouth' (*M&P* 294). Translation becomes a form of ventriloquism, a way of finding one's own voice, an operation of discovery and refinement. A student of the 'Ezruversity', Bunting was influenced by Pound's approach to translation both as a linguistic act in itself, a way of Making New, and as a discipline in its own right where exposure to other languages turned the poet into a cultural negotiator. Bunting's translations reveal range and give us a particular insight into his poetry. Pound's *Homage to Sextus Propertius*, which is particularly attentive to atmosphere and insists on the need for 'real speech in the English version', is an emblematic example of such an approach (*PBB* 110). Bunting also rated the poem's musical quality highly.[10] We have seen how, as a working principle, Bunting appropriates and co-opts texts by means of translation and adaptation in the formulation of his poems in general. A checklist of the collected and uncollected Overdrafts lays out a set of names that have variously and often quite specifically influenced Bunting's poetry: Lucretius, Horace, Catullus, Firdosi, Rudaki, Manuchehri, Sa'di and Hafiz.

The earlier Overdrafts sometimes have a laboratorial feel, especially when he is working in Latin. The reader can see this in 'Verse and Version' (*CP* 152), Bunting's translation of Zukofsky *into* Latin; whilst a piece on Catullus ends with dramatic italic emphasis *'and why Catullus bothered to write pages and pages of this drivel mystifies me'* (*CP* 153). Early work on Horace (*CP* 150–1), on the other hand, not only shows Bunting engaged with characteristic Horatian economy, it reveals the manner in which the classical piece is modernized by idiomatic English. Eros, as ever, provides distractions:

Minerva

's not at all pleased that your seam's dropped for a fair sight
of that goodloooking athlete's wet shoulders

when he's been swimming and stands
    towelling himself in full view
of the house.

(CP 150)

With similar linguistic quickness the next piece opens: 'Please stop gushing about his pink/neck smooth arms and so forth, Dulcie; it makes me sick' (*CP* 151). Bunting maintained: 'Every revivification of poetry has taken the same route, towards the language of the street and the cadences of song or bodily movement' (*M&P* 236). His first collected Overdraft (CP 149), written in 1927, is likewise revealing. The opening lines are from *De Rerum Natura*, a text that from the beginning was of importance to Bunting: Lucretius 'is almost the only poet, except recently Hugh MacDiarmid, to make poetry out of scientific lingo, there is both a vividness in his description [...] and a splendid dignity on the rare occasions where he breaks off to address the reader or the gods'.[11] In Bunting's address to Venus we note, in the name of concision and musicality, that the original is shortened from twenty-five to eighteen lines, a clear demonstration of the poet's condensing strategy. It seems apposite, too, that he should begin his career as translator addressing the goddess of love:

> Darling of Gods and Men, beneath the gliding stars
> you fill rich earth and buoyant sea with your presence
> for every living thing achieves its life through you.
>
> (*CP* 149)

The Latin piece allows Bunting to conflate Lucretian agnosticism with Wordsworthian wonder. 'Tintern Abbey' works towards a similar position: 'with an eye made quiet by the power/ Of harmony, and the deep power of joy,/ We see into the life of things.' *Briggflatts* is habitually mindful of the natural world and it's hard to resist comparing the tenth line of Bunting's translation of Lucretius – 'Then the shy cattle leap and swim the brooks for love' – with the opening passage of the poem he would write some forty years later (*CP* 61). After celebrating Venus' power, where 'Everywhere, through all seas mountains and waterfalls,/love caresses all hearts and kindles all creatures', the goddess is apostrophized at the end of the poem: 'Alma Venus! *Trim my poetry*/with your grace; and give peace to write and read and think.' (my italics) Even at this early stage, through the medium of translation, Bunting is underlining the importance of concision and economy.

There is a rewarding overlap between the development of

Bunting's poetic in general and his engagement with foreign models of poetry. The Horatian ode leans, for example, on the Buntingian ode and we find in this later piece a recapitulation of the mortality drama which is evident throughout Bunting's writing:

> You can't grip years, Postume,
> that ripple away nor hold back
> wrinkles and, soon now, age,
> nor can you tame death.

(CP 161)

If Horace is the Latin poet who most exercises Bunting in the Overdrafts, collected and uncollected, it's important to make a distinction between the classical translations and his later embrace of Persian poetry. If Firdosi proved to be Bunting's Persian catalyst, the Englishman's extended residence in Iran fostered a rare expertise. Parvin Loloi and Glyn Pursglove remind us that 'The relationship between the Latin and English languages and between the two literary traditions is, of course, a long and intimate one', whereas the relationship between the English and Persian traditions is 'much briefer and more eccentric'. The translation of Persian poetry into English has long been associated with Edward Fitzgerald whose *The Rubáiyát of Omar Khayyám* is now seen as an example of nineteenth-century Orientalism. 'Latin may be a dead language for most of us in the West', continue Loloi and Pursglove, 'but Persian is simply unknown to us.' In their discussion of Bunting's Persian Overdrafts, they draw our attention to Persian forms and structures – the *bait, qasida, rubai, ghazal* – and demonstrate how in avoiding mechanical rhyme Bunting finds an English-sounding idiom without disguising 'the poetry's rhetorical bases'. They argue that although 'The formal qualities of the originals are naturally lost', Bunting 'offers us in their place English poetry of a high order.' Not only are his Persian translations a considerable achievement, they make a major 'but neglected contribution to the scanty tradition of distinguished English translations of Persian poetry' (*M&P* 353).

We have noted how the translation of Rudaki (*CP* 155) feeds into Bunting's writings about the passing of time where the body itself becomes the site of crisis. Several of the uncollected

Overdrafts, in particular, give rise to chutzpah on the part of Bunting. He begins a piece by Sa'di: 'Many well-known people have been packed away in cemeteries' (*CP* 204), reminding us of his line in *Briggflatts*: 'There's a lot of Italy in churchyards' (*CP* 67). And Bunting takes the liberty of transforming the thirteenth-century Sufi poet Hafiz, whose verse celebrates the numinous effects of wine, into a twentieth-century *poète maudit*. Interestingly, Bunting takes the title from Catullus' Poem 8 for this translation (*CP* 206) – '*Desinas ineptire*' ('Stop acting Foolishly'). In effect, Bunting reads Catallus to read Hafiz so that Bunting's Hafiz 'is recast in the mode of Bunting's conception of Catallus' which means that 'Hafiz is given the directness and the erotic passion of the Roman poet and stripped of his mysticism.'[12]

> Give respectability and pride the go-by, *Hafiz*,
> cadge yourself a drop of booze and get
> > crapulously drunk.
>
> (*CP* 206)

Manuchehri is the source of several glorious poems: 'Night is hard by, I am vexed and bothered by sleep./Dear my girl, bring me something to cure me of sleep' (*CP* 213). Or another which begins 'You, with my enemy, strolling down my street/you're a nice one!' (*CP* 214), or the exuberant

> Hi, tent-boy, get that tent down.
> The first are gone and one drum's growled,
> loads on the camels, nearly prayer-time,
> and tonight full moon.
>
> (*CP* 216)

Persian poets provided Bunting with a palette which was both extravagant and exquisite. He learnt from them the intimacies of verbal patterning which later fed into *Briggflatts*. In their discussion of Bunting's translations of Hafiz, Parvin Loloi and Glyn Pursglove explain how in Persian poetics 'a *ghazal* has traditionally been compared to a pearl necklace, to which each *bait* [similar to a couplet] contributes a perfect pearl [...] It will be noted that the metaphor of the necklace implies circularity; the *ghazal* is envisaged not so much as a *sequence* of "thoughts" but rather as a pattern of images which has much in common with other characteristically Persian art forms' (*M&P* 191). These include 'Persian architecture (the central court-yard), garden-layout (the medial pool), carpet-design, mosaics and minia-tures'.[13] If Persian poetry offers a range of textual and tonal possibilities, Bunting's feisty appropriation and colloquial drive and his stepping away from 'mystical sensibility' re-make the poems according to his own criteria and create a twentieth-century directness.[14] If Bunting attends to the spirit of the original, his Overdrafts show that he is firmly at the helm, reminding us of his editorial note, 'It would be gratuitous to assume that a mistranslation is unintentional' (CP 228), and likewise affirming his argument that 'A good translator intends to make the same impression on his readers as the original poet made on his' (SV 64). I will finish by quoting Bunting's translation of Sa'di:

> Last night without sight of you my brain was ablaze.
> My tears trickled and fell plip on the ground. That I with
> sighing might bring my life to a close they would name
> you and again and again speak your name till
> with night's coming all eyes closed save mine whose every
> hair pierced my scalp like a lancet. That was
> not wine I drank from your sight but my heart's
> blood gushing into the cup. Wall and door wherever
> I turned my eyes scored and decorated with shapes
> of you. To dream of Laila Majnun prayed for
> sleep. My senses came and went but neither your
> face saw I nor would your fantom go from me.
> Now like aloes my heart burned, now smoked as a censer.
> Where was the morning gone that used on other nights
> to breathe till the horizon paled? Sa'di!
> Has then the chain of the Pleiades broken
> tonight that every night is hung on the sky's neck?

(CP 160)

6

Briggflatts

All roads lead to *Briggflatts*. If Bunting's great poem is 'the song of a Modernist "Viking", plunderer of experience, who chooses freedom instead of "hearth,"'[1] it is also the song of the poet-traveller who comes to understand, like the eighteenth-century explorer John Ledyard, the etymological overlap between 'errant' and 'error'[2] and yearns for the 'reek of [the] hearth's scent' and the nourishment of 'sour rye porridge from the hob' (*CP* 63). The long journey behind the poem's creation, as we have seen, creates a compelling narrative. 'The art of reading', argues Michael Schmidt, 'like that of writing requires perspective, establishing a certain distance from one's own language, one's own concerns, even one's own community or country [. .] For Basil Bunting the distance was found in long exile – on the Continent, in contact with Yeats and Pound, with sullen diplomats and ambitious military officers in Persia – and in his pacifism during the First World War.'[3] *Briggflatts*, written in the 1960s, is, in effect, a literary *nostos*, a Northumbrian home-coming, what Herbert Read called 'a poem of return [...] after long sojourns in exotic lands' (*PBB* 213). James McGonigal argues: 'Here was a link not only with the great poetic generation but also with a life of restless literary wandering, Goliardic, heedless of reputation, at once disturbing and attractive.'[4] He continues: 'Whereas Yeats sailed to Byzantium, so to speak, Bunting sailed back.'[5] He brought with him a great deal of literary cargo. *Briggflatts* can be seen as a form of geographical and cultural *translation* in which the fragments, texts and languages of a long poetic life are converted into this lifelong poem creating not only a type of elegy but, according to Edward Lucie-Smith, an elegy 'for the poet's own life'[6] in which 'the star you steer by is gone'. In part *Briggflatts* is an act of retrieval. 'It is easier to die than to remember', we are told, but the poem, with its Wordsworthian spots of time, *does* remember, binding the sheets and indexing the volume against the poet's ruins.

The journeying forth in order to journey back, which describes the Odyssean trajectory of Bunting's *Briggflatts*, is a journey back to Northumbria. Donald Davie, who was zealous about Bunting's poem, was a Yorkshire poet who regarded the north of England as a litmus test for a kind of cultural authenticity. In *Six Epistles to Eva Hesse*, a long address in rhyming couplets to Pound's German translator, Davie contrasts the relationship between Poundian mythopoetry and Charles Olson's Projective Verse with an intrinsically empirical English poetic which is bound by the modest and *measurable* landscape of an exiguous island. He invokes the 'potent lexicon/Of place' and argues that 'being English helps with this' claiming as his emblem 'tiny Hugsett, where we would /Cull bluebells forty years ago'. For Davie 'place (*all* places)' are 'holy', upholding Williams' belief that the local is the true expression of the universal and supporting Charles Tomlinson's assertion in 'The Return' that 'place is always an embodiment/And incarnation beyond argument'.[7] The *Six Epistles* anticipates Davie's return to England after many years in America and for all his fluency and sympathy with the international scope of modernism he explains how 'some lump of English clay' ultimately 'grounds' him.[8] Davie describes *Briggflatts* 'as a poem in celebration of Northumbria, a region historically larger than, but centred on, the poet's native Northumberland to which he had retuned after a nomadic life spent mostly in foreign parts, particularly in the Middle East'. He continues: 'The deeply ingrained English-ness of *Briggflatts* has to be insisted on, because British insularity has sometimes tried to push Bunting into the margin by representing him as rootless cosmopolitan.'[9]

That 'ingrained Englishness' – northern Englishness – is woven in the title of the poem itself where Brigflatts[10] is the name of a hamlet in the Pennine mountains near Sedbergh in Cumbria which Bunting first visited as a 13-year-old schoolboy at the invitation of his school friend John Greenbank. John's sister Peggy would eventually become the dedicatee of *Brigg-flatts*, making the poem a romance spanning some fifty years.

Peggy Greenbank's father was a stone mason and the reader can see, especially in the opening section of the poem, how romantic-erotic recollections of Brigflatts *the place* nourish *Briggflatts* the literary work. The Quaker meeting house at Brigflatts, built in 1675, has its own numinosity and one notes how an English locality, wedded to the traditions of Non-conformism, permeates the atmosphere of the poem.

Michael Hamburger has written of 'Bunting's highly developed sense of place, and of particular ways of life rooted in particular localities'.[11] *Briggflatts* is attentive to cultural and spiritual geographies: Italy, the Canaries, the Middle East, Northumbria, London, Rapallo, Isfahan, Brigflatts. The 'montage of places' in Bunting's poem underscores the uniqueness of place itself.[12] The crossover from the Arabic/Persian into Early English/Celtic culture is inscribed in the intricate craftsmanship of the *Codex Lindisfarnensis* whose 'plaited lines' and calligraphy are part of the unifying design of the poem.

I will return to the significance of the Quaker tradition in relation to Bunting's poem, yet from the beginning it is important to acknowledge how *Briggflatts* explores both the profane and the sacred, how in both its larger structures and at a micro-level, the poem effects transitions and contrasts between hell-like degradation and the Edenic. In the earlier Sonatas we have seen how Bunting makes the hell/paradise binary central to his sometimes vitriolic enquiries and that binary is reconfigured in *Briggflatts*. Instead of Yeatsian rage, Bunting suggests the possibility of a healing acceptance: 'Old age can see at last the loveliness of things overlooked or despised, frost, the dancing maggots, sheepdogs, and particularly the stars which make time a paradox and a joke until we can give up our own time, even though we wasted it' (NB). Pound's spiritual charge came from the classical gods: 'Given the material means', he claimed, 'I would replace the statue of Venus on the cliffs of Terracina, I would erect a temple to Artemis in Park Lane.'[13] Bunting eschews the monumental and the hieratic and locates the source of his spirituality in the modesty of a Quaker meeting house in a named English hamlet.

Briggflatts is both a 'Wordsworthian' process of recollection and a travelogue in which a 'Romantic' poem is couched in modernist form where 'The narrator awakens into identity through a childhood sexual encounter; the girl he lies with is like Wordsworth's Lucy, an embodiment of the land.'[14] R. S. Woof suggests that 'the children's love-making has a touch of a Cathy and a Heathcliff who have read their D. H. Lawrence.'[15] The poem begins and ends in the north of England and Bunting's wanderings are threaded into the text. The journeying out in order to journey back is captured in the narratorial arc of the poem but any would-be linearity is collapsed into sonata form. The musicality of the piece – the laying of 'the tune on the air' – enacts both conflation and juxtaposition, where seasonal progression, romance and myth create the sense of a mini epic or epyllion. Its musical order takes its bearings from Scarlatti's B minor fugato sonata (*PBB* 210). Specific localities and named places are characteristic of Bunting's writing, ensuring that the poet's border crossings are marshalled into concrete presentation. Timothy Clark argues that Bunting's poetry is representative of those British poets of modernist sympathy who affirm 'local environments with cosmopolitan eyes'.[16]

> Brag, sweet tenor bull,
> descant on Rawthey's madrigal.

> (*CP* 61)

Much is prefigured in the opening of *Briggflatts*: the presence of the Throckley bull, which later fuses into the story of Pasiphae, the heralding of poetry as music, the economy of poetic delivery, the River Rawthey, analogous with Wordsworth's Derwent in *The Prelude*, where both rivers connote a recognizable geography. Named places and named people, including Eric Bloodaxe, the murdered Viking warrior-king, weave themselves into the texture of the poem. Garsdale, Hawes, Stainmore evoke a Viking history, a northern dialect and a layered geological landscape where 'their becks ring on limestone,/ whisper to peat' (*CP* 62).

Section Two takes us away from rural Northumbria to the London of the 1920s. The metropolis, as we have seen in earlier poems, has Dantean accents and the poet 'Secret, solitary, a spy' now walks 'among the bogus'. We are returned to the poet's youthful stomping grounds – 'bus conductor/against engine against wheels against/the pedal, Tottenham Court Road, decodes/thunder' (*CP* 65) – and we are taken back to Papa

Kleinfeldt's Fitzroy Tavern, once Bunting's drinking haunt and the 'Rendezvous of all the World' (*PS* 23). Section Two, the London interlude aside, acknowledges the poet's 'Italian period' whose 'Flying Fish follow[ing] the boat/delicate wings blue' evoke Pound's 'the flying azure of the wing'd fish under Zoagli' (*Canto* LXXV1). Images of Italy are various and there are Ligurian reminiscences too.[17] We see the narrator negotiating la Cisa crossing between the Ligurian and Tuscan Apennines and recalling the 'marine olives and hillside/blue figs, under the breeze fresh/with pollen of Apennine sage' (*CP* 67). We move quickly between Orvieto, Lucca, Amalfi and Parma as well as the landscapes of the Garfagnana and the Apuan Alps whose 'White marble stained like a urinal' recalls the lapidary endeavours of the stone mason in Section One and looks forward to the 'glazed crag' in Section Three. Here, in what becomes the poem's architectural apex, Alexander encounters Israfel the Angel of Death with 'trumpet in hand'. Stainmore, the place of Bloodaxe's murder, is referred to again in the second section but the Asian vultures which ride 'on a spiral/ column of dust' (*CP* 69), an image that might have come from *The Spoils*, prefigure the eastern landscape of Section Three.

If the heroics and failures of Bloodaxe feature in the first two sections, the third section focuses on Alexander the Great ('He went far beyond the flaming walls of the world', *PBB* 210). Bunting steps back into Firdosi's *Shahnameh* and draws on the early Persian account of Alexander's wandering 'through country after country where the most horrible things are going on, and ultimately comes to the mountains of Gog and Magog on the edge of the world'. Bunting continues: 'All alone he climbs up to the top of the mountain, and there he sees the angel sitting exactly as in my poem, with the trumpet ready to his lips to blow, and looking anxiously to the east for the signal to blow [. . .] and put an end to the world'.[18] Alexander ceases his questing and leads his troops back to Macedonia. After this retreat from the brink of hubris, Alexander/Bunting is addressed by the emblematic slowworm. Side-stepping the mythical possibilities of snake and lizard, the narrator/slowworm presents a strategy of lesser visibility, of keeping one's head down, a strategy learnt from a lifetime of combative experiences, the fulfilment of the 'humble, concrete [and the] lived' (*SV* 320):

I am neither snake nor lizard,
I am the slowworm.

(CP 73)

The slowworm is rather like the poet as spy:

> I prosper
> lying low, little concerned.
> My eyes sharpen
> when I blink.

(CP 73)

Anti-heroic, if charismatic, the slowworm becomes the unlikely monarch of Bunting's generously apportioned animal kingdom and 'the slowworm's song' graces the poem's musical ensemble.

Section Four lists ancient warrior-poets and early medieval religious figures, including the all-important St Cuthbert, Bishop of Lindisfarne. The geography – Teesdale and Wensleydale – as well as the historical narratives are emphatically northern. Makin writes about this with impressive detail (*SV* 160–215), and the long solemn opening of Section Four acts as a kind of palimpsest whose narratorial centre hovers between the sixth and seventh centuries and which serves as a general reminder of how 'Today's posts are piles to drive into the quaggy past' (*CP* 75) hence re-affirming Pound's ahistorical assertion that 'all ages are contemporaneous', yet also revealing an innate sympathy for exotic, northern histories. This post-Roman period, some three centuries before the exploits of Eric Bloodaxe, is habitually, if erroneously, described as the Dark Ages. The challenge to that description is found in various Anglo-Saxon/Celtic artefacts, one of the most famous of which is the Lindisfarne Gospels whose intricate patterning and arabesque design serves as a model for Bunting's poem, as well as grounding *Briggflatts* into a specific cultural geography. The reference to Aneurin the bard, ascribed the authorship of the *Gododdin*, as well as the citing of the Welsh poet Taliesin, whose name has entered Arthurian mythology, inject an epic dimension which informs the poem generally and which likewise sets up a heroic dynamic against which the epicurean slowworm creates its own pragmatic antidote. This section is not without its hieratic tones recalling a bardic-oral tradition which, in turn, challenges the ascendancy of the post-1945 Movement with its lowered sights and suburban visions: 'Aneurin and Taliesin, cruel owls/for whom it is never altogether dark, crying/before the ruled made poetry a pedant's game' (*CP* 75). Bunting's inclusion of post-Roman histories, Anglo-Saxon, Cymric-Celtic, Viking, not to mention traces of early Islamic culture, has a double effect. Not only does it lay down the foundations of a fierce localism, where history stretches into the shadow of mythology, but it also reminds us of the intercultural richness of early British history. Kingsley Amis called for an embargo on poems about 'mythology or foreign cities or other poems'; Bunting breaks free from the insularity of Little-Englandism by the rendering of English history itself.

Section Five heralds the Northumbrian homecoming in several ways, not least in its recollection of amorous encounters with Peggy Greenbank at Brigflatts some fifty years beforehand. The final forty-five lines, where 'Orion strides over Farne' (*CP* 80) reach for and achieve an emotional climax which sees the marshalling of planetary constellations, hard-won yet consoling memory and an impressive lyrical quickening to affirm the past in the present. The repeated 'Then is Now' qualifies the earlier 'It is easier to die than to remember' (*CP* 64). Yet rather in the way that the embattled salmon, seasoned now rather than 'unseasonable', turns the triumph of its homecoming into its own demise, Bunting's poem clinches its erotic and literary fulfilment at the very moment it conjures up Catullus' *Nox est perpetua una dorminienda*. The temptations of transcendence are reined in, however, by the determined use of named places. *Briggflatts* has provided a litany of names and here towards the end of the poem Bunting draws on his memories of living in a shepherd's dwelling in the late 1920s:

> fell-born men of precise instep
> leading demure dogs
> from Tweed and Till and Teviotdale,
> with hair combed back from the muzzle,
> dogs from Redesdale and Coquetdale
> taught by Wilson or Telfer.

(CP 79)

Bunting has argued 'things noticed for the first time

especially, are particularly vivid, they come over much better to the reader than any abstraction',[19] and Herbert Read sees the poem as affecting 'a series of first impressions' (*PBB* 217), even if, as a 'connoisseur of etymological depth', the poet-mason also creates a poem of lapidary force.[20] Never 'a book-bug cooped in a study' (*SV* 271), Bunting affirms William Carlos Williams' *obiter dicta* 'No ideas but in things' and celebrates the lived and *experienced* which, notwithstanding the poet's wariness of theory, becomes a form of Romantic Empiricism. Shepherds are never without mythological potential, but in a poem that sometimes reads like a code, these are *Northumbrian* shepherds.

The skill of *Briggflatts* lies in the holding together of various narratives and motifs. By the end of the poem, Bunting's longest and most ambitious sonata, the poet has taken us back to an erotic yet prelapsarian moment which celebrates 'Peggy Greenbank and her whole ambience, the Rawthey valley, the fells of Lunedale, the Viking inheritance all spent save the faint smell of it [and] the ancient Quaker life accepted without thought and without suspicion that it might seem eccentric.' And, in this revealing letter to Zukofsky, Bunting also considers 'What happens when one deliberately thrusts love aside, as I then did – it has its revenge' (*PBB* 207). During one of their holidays together the teenage couple slipped into the meeting house and conducted an unofficial Quaker marriage ceremony (*PS* 13). Not only an act of remembrance, *Briggflatts* also becomes a kind of epithalamium manqué or a renewal of the 'wedding vows' which had been undertaken in adolescent solemnity/jest. Hence, the poem attempts to right a wrong or heal a broken love-line, to undo the 'Love murdered' and 'love laid aside' (Section One) and now, in effect, reply to 'a letter unanswered' and make good that 'visit postponed for fifty years' (Section Five). Regret and intimations of mortality, which co-opt Cavalcanti's 'No hope of going back', and where the murder of Eric Bloodaxe has become a tangible example of the wrong road taken, are finessed by erotic memory. 'Gentle generous voices weave/over bare night/words to confirm and delight/till bird dawn' (*CP* 63) to create a delicate aubade in which the young lovers acknowledge the end of night, anticipating the second aubade of Section Four where 'her blanket comforts my belly like the south', and where '[They] have eaten and loved and the sun is up./Goodbye' (*CP* 76). This, in effect, prepares us for the half-conceit at the end of the poem. In 'To his Coy Mistress' Andrew Marvell cajoles the reticent woman by reminding her that 'The grave's a fine and private place/But none I think do there embrace.' In Catullus' address to Lesbia (Catullus 5), the Roman poet similarly encourages love's embrace because the extinguishing of light leaves only un-broken night. *Lux* and *Nox* are set up as irreconcilable opposites, yet Walter Raleigh's translation of the poem where 'after our short light' we sleep 'one everlasting night' might also be imagining the deferred erotic possibilities of endless night. In his discussion of Bunting the poet-wanderer who rejects woman for the open road, Dennis Brown imagines that Julia Kristeva 'might construe this as a masculist choice of Thanatos over Eros'.[21] Yet the end of *Briggflatts* might be seen as the collapsing of Thanatos *into* Eros where the interruption of night seen in Section One now becomes 'uninterrupted night', a form of counter-aubade where starlight, which was 'almost flesh', discovers its own quickening. At the end of *Briggflatts* the night is flecked by light:

> Starlight quivers. I had day enough.
> For love uninterrupted night.

> (*CP* 80)

And the Coda, too, with its nautical imagery and gnomic resonance, shies away from eschatological certainty even as it takes us back to the execution of Bloodaxe: 'And still we know neither where we are nor why' muses Bunting in a note on the poem (NB). The poem leaves us with this philosophical withholding:

> Where we are who knows
> of kings who sup
> while day fails? Who,
> swinging his axe
> to fell kings, guesses
> where we go?

> (*CP* 81)

The progress of the poem's narrative of love, from Section One where the poet-narrator 'has untied the tape of her [the girl's] striped flannel drawers/before the range' and where

96

'Naked/on the pricked rag mat/his fingers comb/thatch of his manhood's home' (*CP* 63) to Section Five where 'light from the zenith/spun when the slowworm lay in her lap/fifty years ago'(*CP* 80), is framed by the cycle of the seasons. Spring contains its own 'cruelty' in which the stone-mason recalls funereal rites and (Section Two) where 'A disappointed July full of codling/moth and ragged lettuces' prepares us for the hell-like third section where 'One /plucked fruit warm from the arse/ of his companion' and where 'beggars advertise /rash, chancre, fistula' (*CP* 72). The movement into autumn and winter provides its own *memento mori* yet also takes us further from corrupted images of fecundity and garners many of the poem's poetic highpoints. The emergence of Sirius at the poem's end after the winter solstice – the dog star typically associated with summer heat – reconfigures the Then is Now and reminds us that although the stars are part of the sailors' almanac they are now 'beyond chronological compass' (*CP* 80), one of several instructions within the poem that warn us against applying a linear reading to the work. All of this is buttressed by the *failures* of Bloodaxe and Alexander and a small army of saints. The most significant of these is Cuthbert whose embrace of the animal world feeds into the poem's ecological currents.

Bunting, of course, resisted the exegetical process – 'There is no excuse for literary criticism' – and the reader is forewarned in Section Four: 'Follow the clue patiently and you will understand nothing' (*CP* 75). The shepherds in the final section might 'follow the links' but the mail of Bloodaxe has been loaded with 'linked lies' (Section Two), and the pubescent lovers' voices 'weave/over bare night' (Section One), reminding us of the spider's shadowy 'web' (Section Two) which recalls the flying fish with their 'Flexible, unrepetitive line' (Section One). The patterning replicates the designs which 'punctuate a text whose initial' is 'lost in Lindisfarne plaited lines' and which 'stands for discarded love' (Section Two). Bunting has spoken with passion about The Lindisfarne Book.[22] The Northumbrian text threaded its way into the composition of *Briggflatts*.[23] The seventh-century manuscript draws on Roman, Byzantine, Celtic and Teutonic traditions and the 'cross-carpet' pages reflect the oriental rugs and prayer-mats of Islamic design which meant, in effect, that Bunting was able to take his Arabic/Persian scholarship back to

Northumbria in a quite tangible manner. Bunting the craftsman describes poetry as 'a skill like weaving carpets' (*PBB* 252). This dynamic works against linearity in favour of a circular or maze effect, where the poet-narrator sometimes merges with the poem's protagonists, and where autobiographical matter is never solipsistic. Pasiphae's copulation with the bull evokes the Cretan labyrinth in which the Minotaur was installed. In Bunting's co-opting of musical form, this becomes 'Schoenberg's maze'.

Bunting argues that poetry seeks 'to make not meaning, but beauty' and that meaning is released in the patterns of sound (S). The interconnected designs which characterize the Lindisfarne Gospels are analogous with the 'incremental repetition of themes and recurrent motifs, contrasting rhythms, tempos and texture of sounds, and tone colour' in *Briggflatts* (*PBB* 251). This sonic-visual patterning drives the poem and underlines the poet's belief that music and poetry are closely intertwined, and that 'as soon as you begin to part them things begin to go wrong'.[24] *Briggflatts*, in effect, becomes its own magnificent orchestra and readers should make it their business *to listen* to Bunting's recordings of the poem which bring out the (Old English) alliterative force, where assonance and the smack of consonants not only work on the ear but create the taste of language in the mouth: 'It tastes good' and 'It sounds right' (*CP* 67). Sometimes the music comes from the world around us – the sound of a mallet, 'lark's twitter', the cry of the kittiwake – and sometimes it comes from named composers: Byrd, Monteverdi, Schoenberg and Scarlatti. Bunting's indebtedness to the latter has been widely acknowledged. In Section Four, as the poem's pulse quickens, the acknowledgement is revealing:

> As the player's breath warms the fipple the tone clears.
> It is time to consider how Domenico Scarlatti
> condensed so much music into so few bars
> with never a crabbed turn or congested cadence,
> never a boast or a see-here; and stars and lakes
> echo him and the copse drums out his measure.

(*CP* 76)

It's a key passage, preparing the reader for the biblical cadences of the next stanza ('My love is young but wise'), and underpinning the notion that *Briggflatts* is essentially a *performative* experience. If Eliot's *Four Quartets* stands at some remove behind the musical structure of *Briggflatts*, Mottram notes that in some performances of Bunting's poem the poet had Scarlatti's harpsichord sonatas played alongside the reading.[25] Poetry 'must arise', argues Bunting, 'from the grunts and cries of the dancers',[26] and whilst Scarlatti suggests baroque harmonies, Bunting's orchestra also evokes the dissonant power of modernist music – 'sharing an ear with jazz-men, and with early Stravinsky, or Antheil, or Bartok.' Brown argues that Bunting's lines 'share a world with the *Rite of Spring* or Messiaen's *Turangalilia*' creating 'a truly modernized lyricism', another example of making new.[27] The acknowledgement of Scarlatti cited above has a meta-poetic dimension, an announcement within the text that Bunting's method is also a *condensing* method, 'a plea for conciseness',[28] and a quest for a poem whose form is indivisible from content. Roger Guedalla, Bunting's bibliographer, maintains that 'the poem was written, so Bunting has wryly suggested, to show Tom Pickard how to write a long poem. It was originally 15,000 lines long and was reduced to its final 700 lines over a long period of time.'[29] Bunting's methodology is one of drafts, cuts and exclusions – 'Brief words are hard to find/shapes to carve and discard' (*CP* 64) – creating the resonance of 'a shrunken epic'.[30] Pound lamented towards the end of the *Cantos* that he could not make it cohere. Repeating motifs and creating symmetries, *Briggflatts* seeks its own cohesion, without letting up on its rigorous demands:

> It looks well on the page, but never
> well enough. Something is lost
> when wind, sun, sea upbraid
> justly an unconvinced deserter.

> (*CP* 67)

The dexterity of *Briggflatts* is revealed in the epigraph. We are told that it is an 'Autobiography' for Peggy and we recognize how Bunting has converted fifty years of experience into the poem, even if the writing stays clear of confessional declaration. Bunting maintains that 'My Autobiography is *Briggflatts* – there's nothing else worth speaking aloud' (D). He hasn't observed Eliot's *obiter dicta* regarding the notion of impersonality in any extreme sense yet he has created a poetic vehicle that subsumes personality and creates literary form rather than 'a record of [autobiographical] fact' (*CP* 226). Never solipsistic, Bunting's method is typically allusive, often drawing on his skill as a translator. We find in the epigraph a quotation from the thirteenth-century Spanish text *Libro de Alexandre* – '*Son los pasariellos del mal pelo exidos*' – which not only prefigures the role of Alexander the Great in the poem but also shows how Bunting nuances autobiographical writing with a 'diachronic intertextuality [characterizing] the poetic tradition'.[31] Cannily, the Spanish is translated into contemporary idiom: 'The spuggies are fledged'. Bunting's note explains that 'spuggies' is a Northumbrian word for little sparrows (*CP* 226). The translation of the medieval Spanish into contemporary northern English underscores the Then is Now and gives the poem a northern accent even before it gets under way.[32] Davie draws attention to Bunting's pronunciation of the hard *g* in *spuggies*, heralding the northernness in the sound of the word, and reminding 'Southrons' that the delivery of *Briggflatts*, comes with a Northumbrian pronunciation.[33] Richard Caddel and Anthony Flowers point out that Bunting's pronunciation reveals a Throckley dialect, with its rolling 'r's and linguistic archaisms: 'The accent which Bunting carried with him all his life is thus evidently the highly specific, local language from the place where, and the people amongst whom, he spent his childhood.'[34] The poem's localism is inscribed in the epigraph itself.

This is not to deny the poem's mythic/epic dimension, yet *Briggflatts* is at its most expressive when it grounds the language into locality and when it celebrates 'the inexhaustible plenitude of particulars *in nature*' (*M&P* 168). This is emblematic of how Bunting steps away from Pound's mythopoeic schema as well as Eliotic transcendence and finds an 'English' solution in measurable verities. 'Hierarchy and order, the virtues of the neo-Platonic religion [are] not virtues to me', Bunting was to declare in 'A Note on *Briggflatts*' and he maintained that 'science teaches a respect for fact that no one concerned with making an honest report on things can be without' (*M&P* 234). In effect, 'There is no more fundamentally anti-Platonist view of things than Darwin's' (*SV* 277). Bunting recalls, when a child, a house overrun with lizards as his father, examined the world with

100

microscopic precision. Bunting junior acquired this knack for exactitude. Bunting liked describing things he could see which is quite different from 'hunting for objective correlatives' (*M&P* 269). He combines a Darwinian reflex with a sympathy for the classical philosopher Lucretius who sets about explaining 'the world an atom at a time' (NB). Thom Gunn is impressed by the precision of Bunting's description of the shepherds and their dogs in Section Five: 'every moment described, has the easy *exactness* of familiar recurrence – the turf *studded* with the herb thrift, men of *precise* instep, dogs with *accurate* lips [...] Bunting's comparison of the dogs' teeth to the colour of birchbark is as much a matter of course as the dogs' relation to their masters and to the sheep. It takes genius to recognize the interrelatedness of the scene but, once it is recognized, in a sense all else is found.'[35]

This creates a type of *ecopoeisis*. *Villon*, as early as 1925, had revealed an awareness of nature's fragility in the face of utilitarianism and human greed. In *Briggflatts*, Bunting 'traces the complex web of relations between things' in an eco-system of animals, vegetation and landscape.[36] *Briggflatts* provides its own poetic bestiary where humble gnat, denigrated louse and 'cannibal slug' co-exist with Northumbrian bull and talismanic slowworm, where frogs and grasshoppers inhabit the same textual world as tortoise, conger, sleeping bass and rock lichen and where the agency of the animal world is manifested in the woodman's dazed response to the 'adder's sting' (CP 73). The stylized depictions of animal life in the *Codex Lindisfarnensis* are now realized in the environmental dynamic of *Briggflatts*. The cormorant, frequently depicted in the medieval manuscript, is now brought into Bunting's text:

> but thin light lays
> white next red on sea-crow wing,
> gruff sole cormorant
> whose grief turns carnival.

(CP 78)

Wesling underscores this phenomenological dynamic by arguing that 'In Bunting's world a slowworm, a bough, "A thrush in the syringa" can possess *vox articulata* and enter dialogue with each other and with us.'[37]

Wordsworth's 'looking into the nature of things' stands alongside Bunting's Darwinism, yet whilst the Romantic poet sought 'beyond the things themselves towards a transcendental signified',[38] Bunting's genius lies in the celebration of diversity whose 'scientific accuracy' is cemented 'in the surface detail' of his writing.[39] This creates, at moments, its own carnivalesque democracy. The poem's radical spirit reveals itself in Bunting's engagement with the natural world. 'Could the poet', asks Jonathan Bate, 'be a keystone sub-species of *Homo sapiens*? The poet: an apparently useless creature, but potentially the saviour of ecosystems.'[40] We might choose to see Bunting as an ecological warrior *avant la lettre*. There's a further political dimension to this. Quartermain argues that 'Official culture has very little room for northern margins' and, in the guise of survival and resistance, 'subject races reject the ideologies which serve to bolster the oppressor's power' by turning against 'abstractions, the metaphysics which justifies their subjugation and the syntax of politics which assure their subjugation.' As a form of resistance in itself the under-dog turns to 'the concrete, the physical, the practical: to the flesh; they resort to fact, to the tangible, to objects. Bunting's poetry is remarkably full of *things*, of *facts*.'[41]

Briggflatts is not a hymn to nature in any orthodox sense but the poem is nevertheless informed by a tangible piety. Cuthbert and the humble slowworm are privileged over the hubristic endeavours of Bloodaxe and Alexander and the poem finds its resolution from *within* a mythology of failure. The poet lays aside truculence in favour of humility, yet there is also fierce pride. After the years of neglect which followed his expulsion from Persia, Bunting taps back into Northumbrian culture to create a poem of alliterative power in which the poet's 'habits of language use, and stories of ancient Welsh and Norse heroes, help to construct Northumbria as a proud and hard kingdom that has understandable attractions in a time when the old industrial basis of the North East's economy has been undermined'.[42] Such regional pride prefigures the depredations of Thatcherite policy in the 1980s, yet Bunting is also conscious of Northumbria's earlier fate. After the Norman Conquest the kingdom of Northumbria 'was governed as a conquered province for five full centuries, constantly repressed by the authorities at York.' Bunting is mindful of political defeat and lingering splendour: 'I think our best hope of an art or a literature of our own does not lie in imitating what has come to us from Rome or Europe or from the South of England, but in trying to discern what is our own, and to develop it and fit it for 20th and 21st century conditions.'[43] The reader is given forewarning of the poem's cultural specificity in the poet's notes: 'The Northumbrian tongue [...] sounds strange to men used to the koine or to Americans who may not know how much Northumberland differs from the Saxon south of England. Southrons would maul the music of many lines in *Briggflatts*' (CP 226).

Bunting's cultural makeup was informed by his Quaker upbringing and the meeting house at Brigflatts, in whose cemetery the poet's ashes were scattered, stands firmly behind the poem. Nonconformist churches tended to establish their spiritual bases far from the centres of power, reinforcing the Quakers' distrust of temporal authority.[44] Davie, who has written extensively about Nonconformist traditions, sees Bunting's poetry 'as a flower of dissenting Protestantism'.[45] He argues that Bunting's Quakerism 'has generally been too little heeded' and that although 'his whisky-drinking and richly vernacular and amorously wide-ranging *persona* may seem to set him outside' the Society of Friends, there is little evidence that Bunting reneged on the Quaker allegiance 'that caused him as an eighteen-year-old to register for military service, precisely to declare himself a conscientious objector and so serve a prison term, thereby earning the enduring respect of Ezra Pound'.[46] This combination of Bohemia and avant-gardism along with Quaker pacifism was part of the complex formation of the youthful poet.

Bunting's schoolboy engagement with the Old Testament made him receptive to Jewish and Islamic traditions and the lyricism of the King James Bible fed into his writing. Bunting's beliefs have an agnostic if pantheistic vein: 'I have no use for religion conceived as church forms [...] but I do believe that there is a possibility of a kind of reverence for the whole creation which I feel we ought to have in our bones.' He continues:

> If the word 'God' is to have any use it must include everything. The only way to know anything is to consider yourself a student of

histology, finding out as much as carefully controlled commonsense can find out about the world. In so doing, you will be contributing to the histology of God. (*M&P* 271)

The poet's demanding eye merges with an uncluttered mind. In 'At Briggflatts meetinghouse' (*CP* 145), we ask 'nothing/but silence':

> I'm a Quaker by upbringing, and fortunately it is a religion with no dogma at all – [...] and I don't have to believe this or that or the other. I think that the real essence of the Quaker business is exactly as it was at the beginning: if you sit in silence, if you empty your head of all the things you usually waste your brain thinking about, there is some faint hope that something, no doubt out of the unconscious or where you will, will appear – just as George Fox would have called it, the voice of God. (*M&P* 271)

He returns to the idea in 'A Note on Briggflatts':

> In silence, having swept dust and litter from our minds, we can detect the pulse of God's blood in our veins, more persuasive than words, more demonstrative than a diagram. That is what a Quaker meeting tries to be, and this is why my poem is called *Briggflatts*.

The cleansed mind slays the 'monster of sterility' which has haunted Bunting's poetry since the 1920s and helps to fashion a poem which is conscious of its own making.[47] 'Furthest, fairest things, stars, free of our humbug' heralds the countdown to the poem's magisterial conclusion, implying with apposite humility a state of erasure in the very act of making: 'The Star you steer by is gone'. The poem creates a sense of completion by locking permanence and evanescence into an exquisite, final reckoning:

> The sheets are gathered and bound,
> the volume indexed and shelved,
> dust on its marbled leaves.
> Lofty, an empty combe,
> silent but for bees.
> Finger tips touched and were still
> fifty years ago.

> (*CP* 80)

7

Critical Perspectives

Davie claimed in 1977 that *Briggflatts* is 'where poetry has got to, it is what English poets must assimilate and go on from'.[1] Since the 1950s, Davie had engaged with home-grown, English traditions and foreign, typically American, models of poetry. His *Purity of Diction in English Verse* (1952) was seen as the Movement's unofficial manifesto and his poetry was represented in Robert Conquest's *New Lines* anthology (1956). The poet-critic's investment in the eighteenth century, with its privileging of craft and rationality, would appear to have made him a natural enemy of modernist experiment. Yet, even before the publication of Conquest's Movement anthology, he was arguing that 'Pound has influenced [him] more deeply and more than any other poet of the present century.'[2] By the end of the 1950s, Davie the Movement insider was considering how the English had set about battening down their shutters. It had now become difficult

> to conceive of or approve any 'tone' that [wasn't] ironical, and ironical in a limited way, defensive and deprecating, a way of looking at ourselves and our pretensions, not a way of looking at the world. Hardly ever did we seem to write our poems out of an idea of poetry as a way of knowing the world we were in, apprehending it, learning it.[3]

After the mystifications of the Yeats-Pound-Eliot line, the Bohemian excesses of Dylan Thomas and the neo-Apocalyptic poets of the 1940s, a period of retrenchment was taking place. Larkin's 'Statement' disparages the modernists' 'myth-kitty' and welcomes a poetry unhindered by allusion. It is a call for a cleansing modesty and the paradigm suited a bankrupt country that was letting go of its imperial ambitions. Inevitably, this turning away from international modernism generated a curtailing Little-Englandism and an inward-looking poetic that appeared to be throwing out the baby with the proverbial bath water. If Movement poetry was wary of pretentiousness and 'cultural window-dressing', it went about setting its house in order by imposing such stringent limitations that it became 'painfully modest in its pretensions' and 'deliberately provincial in its scope' and 'marginal in its importance'.[4]

Reviewing Charles Tomlinson's *Seeing is Believing* in 1959, Davie praises his former student for refusing 'to join the silent conspiracy which now unites all the English poets from Robert Graves down to Philip Larkin [...] the conspiracy to pretend that Eliot and Pound never happened'.[5] Davie's 'defection' from the Movement was not without its paradoxes, yet this engagement with modernism led him to Ezra Pound and the forming of a complex, if fascinating, literary relationship. It began with *Ezra Pound: Poet as Sculptor*, Davie's most incisive study, which was published around the time Bunting was composing *Briggflatts*. Pound had been released from St Elizabeth's in 1958 and Davie's critical appraisal can be seen as part of that gradual rehabilitative process which includes Kenner's all-important *The Pound Era*.

The story of Pound has a bearing on the story of Bunting. We have seen in this study how Bunting's relationship with Pound was both significant and problematic. Notwithstanding their differences, and such differences were ideological, cultural and technical, Bunting would never deny the early debt on his part. His 'On the Fly-Leaf of Pound's Cantos' (1949) compares Pound's monumental work with the Alps, telling the reader 'you will have to go a long way round/if you want to avoid them' (*CP* 132). This is literary criticism and homage of a high order. Makin refers to a visit by Denis Goacher to St Elizabeth's in 1954 during which Pound took out a letter in which Bunting had typed out his 'On the Fly-Leaf of Pound's Cantos'. Pound began to read the poem to Goacher and 'broke down in the middle of it and he couldn't finish it because he was so upset [...] It is not often that one poet gives another poet as great a compliment as that' (*SV* 325). When Bunting left Rapallo in 1933 he wouldn't see his one-time mentor again, yet for a while, correspondence with Dorothy Pound continued after the war. Bunting's literary hiatus in the 1950s/early 1960s, before the publication of *Briggflatts*, meant that contact ceased again and by the time Bunting's career had been resurrected in the 1960s Pound had descended into the long silence of his later years. Notwithstanding, this letter by Pound in 1970 reveals the glimpse of a significant literary hinterland as well as a continuing affection: 'Dear Basil, Thanks for your note from Vancouver. If I had your eye for detail I might have done something decent. Yours E.P.' (*SV* 325)

Although a rather crude analysis there is some usefulness in pegging Bunting's fortunes to the Pound Index. Pound's fall from grace after the Second World War corresponded with Bunting's literary disappearance in the 1950s. Later critical treatment of Pound, which recognized amongst other things his vital role as an impresario for the modernist cause, corresponded with Bunting's rising fortunes in the 1960s. Interestingly, the publication of *Briggflatts* occurred in the same year as Eliot's death. Eliot had put himself at the heart of the British literary establishment, a position he sustained through his all-important editorial role at Faber and Faber. In effect, he generated a *Faberised* version of modernism which, amongst other things, excluded Bunting. Eliot had rejected the Englishman's work in the 1930s and the 1950s. Although the relationship between Eliot and Pound had been crucial in the early years, with Pound playing a key editorial role in the composition of *The Waste Land*, the trajectory of their respective careers had been very different. If Eliot had made himself into the 'acceptable' face of the modernist revolution, Pound remained the ultimate dissident and his later incarceration symbolized his embattled cultural politics. Whereas the *Four Quartets* had brought the post-symbolist tradition of modernist poetics to a close,[6] Pound's inability 'to make it cohere' had created an open poetic wound which encouraged others to try out a range of strategies. Whereas William Carlos Williams responded to *The Waste Land* by saying 'Eliot returned us to the classroom just at the moment when I felt that we were on the point of escape',[7] Pound's *Cantos* created a toolkit which allowed younger poets to experiment. Poundian legacies are variegated and plentiful, the baton handed down the line and sometimes to unexpected runners. His influence can be traced through Zukofsky and the

Objectivists, Charles Olson and Black Mountain poetry, even Ginsberg and the Beats. Poundian poetics and its continuities/displacements, and one remembers that Pound was writing into the 1960s, feeds into a conversation about modernism, neo-modernism, post-modernism and L-A-N-G-U-A-G-E poetry. One could despise his politics and yet be energized by his experimental drive. According to Seed, Bunting did not air his differences with the American poet *in public* and 'remained loyal to Pound as the master craftsman of modern verse'.[8]

Eliot's carefully cultivated narrative of Anglo-American modernist poetics fed into the mainstream, especially in Britain, where Eliot had assiduously transformed himself into an Englishman. Eliot had rejected Bunting's work for being too 'Poundian' and, in effect, it wasn't until the 1960s that Bunting found a British publisher. I have sought to question the extent of Pound's influence on Bunting's later work, yet there was a perception, which in some quarters still remains, that Bunting was 'the only card-carrying English Poundian'.[9] Such a perception could cut both ways and I have suggested that Bunting's position improved generally with the critical rehabilitation of Pound in the 1960s. The Movement's ascendancy in the 1950s, with its anti-modernist reflex, had earlier created a hostile terrain for the reception of Bunting's poetry, where any association with Pound would have been used by the prosecuting counsel. Larkin cited Pound, one of the three 'Ps', as a modernist bogeyman. The American, along with Picasso and Charlie Parker, had, according to Larkin, destroyed the natural contract between artist and non-specialist by putting experimental technique at the heart of their respective projects.[10]

The effects of the Movement, meretricious or otherwise, have been variously documented.[11] Conquest's *New Lines* anthology (1956) became the standard-bearer of an indigenous reaction against international modernism and subsequent anthologies have positioned themselves in relation to Movement and post-Movement orthodoxies. This has resulted in the battle of anthologies in which a highly policed middle ground as well as alternative, experimental traditions are staked out and fought over with no little vitriol. Editorial introductions become manifestos and sometimes, for all the brouhaha, the anthologized poems actually remind us of the poems they are putatively contesting. Alvarez's *The New Poetry* (1962) constitutes, nevertheless, an important post-war critical moment. The focus of its attack is Conquest's *New Lines* which is accused of moral pusillanimity and hence perpetuating the English disease of 'gentility'. Alvarez reminds his readers of recent European history – 'concentration camps run scientifically as death factories' – and calls for a new seriousness in poetry.[12] He turns to the 'confessional' poetic of Berryman, Lowell, Sexton and Plath to inject an American intensity into the anthology. *Briggflatts*, with its 'I hear Aneurin number the dead and rejoice,/being adult male of a merciless species' (*CP* 75), wouldn't be published until 1966 and it's intriguing to consider how Alvarez might have incorporated this decisively non-Movement poem into his argument.

The editors of *The Penguin Book of Contemporary British Poetry* (1982) chose to ignore the British Poetry Revival of the 1960s and 1970s by claiming tendentiously that very little seemed to be happening in the world of poetry during that period. *Briggflatts* is given no mention. Naturally, they were making an ideological argument insofar as the British Poetry Revival was promoting a set of radical and/or international strategies that were seemingly opposed to the provincial agenda of the Movement. In their championing of ludic, post-modern gesture, Blake Morrison and Andrew Motion were reformulating the middle-ground, basically 'the Movement plus visual fireworks'.[13] Their anthology had its detractors, and inspired a set of counter anthologies which included *A Various Art* (1987), *The New British Poetry 1968–88* (1988), *Conductors of Chaos* (1996) and *Other: British and Irish Poetry Since 1970* (1999), as well as Keith Tuma's generously catholic *Anthology of Twentieth-Century British and Irish Poetry* (2001).

In effect, Ian Sinclair's *Conductors of Chaos* evokes and challenges Conquest's call for the players of the 'Id' section to be controlled by an exigent conductor and therefore signals a belated if passionate assault on Movement/post-Movement hegemony. It is fitting that this profoundly anti-Movement text should become a quasi-Blakean apologia for the 'remote, alienated, fractured' and should tip its hat 'to American open-field poetics and European surrealism' and 'the wearied survivors of classical modernism'. Sinclair resurrects and defends a risk-taking, iconoclastic poetry whose practitioners work outside a Movement-driven mainstream and he acknowledges the neo-Apocalyptic poets of the 1940s, J. H. Prynne and the 'Cambridge School' and the forgotten voices that lie behind the British Poetry Revival. Taking no prisoners, Sinclair puts those mainstreamers who have busily constructed their careers 'rummaging through Philip Larkin's bottom drawer' up against the wall. Sinclair's anthology is a high octane, belligerent call for a wider recognition of those poetic traditions that have been side-lined and marginalized by a sometimes narrow mainstream. He beats a loud drum for poetry's outsiders and discontents. Eric Mottram, who had championed Bunting's work, and whose role as a promoter of alternative poetries is referred to below, is given due acknowledgement. Sinclair refers to John Calder's obituary in the *Independent* (19 January, 1995) in which Mottram is described as 'the best-known "unknown" poet in England'.[14]

These arguments are taken up by the editors of *Other*. Although Richard Caddel and Peter Quartermain are providing a critique of British and Irish poetry, their publisher is, revealingly, American. American poetry has provided escape strategies to British poets who feel trapped by insular home-grown orthodoxies. The literary traffic across the Atlantic has long been embedded in our cultural history but the volume of that traffic has depended on an interesting set of contingencies. Keith Tuma raises the stakes by arguing that 'British poetry is dead so long as no British poetry critic seems destined to fill the vacancies left by the deaths of Donald Davie and Eric Mottram, who used to carry the news of recent poetries back and forth across the Atlantic.'[15] Caddel and Quartermain argue that one of the purposes of *Other* is 'to uncover what the forces surrounding the Movement and its successors have helped to bury'.[16] They are particularly exercised by Anthony Thwaite's *Poetry Today: A Critical Guide to British Poetry 1960–1995*. His study, they argue:

> might legitimately be read as representing the dominant 'mainstream' view. In none of its three editions does his book mention such remarkable long modernist works as Brian Coffey's *Advent* (1975), or the work of Basil Bunting (1900–1985), W. S. Graham (1918–1986), and Jonathan Griffin (1906–1990), all actively and influentially writing and publishing through the sixties and

seventies. The book takes no cognizance of ambitious projects like Allen Fisher's *Place* project from the 1970s or Robert Sheppard's ongoing *Twentieth Century Blues*. As Maurice Scully has noted, there is a 'completely buried "modernist/experimental" tradition.' [17]

Whereas Bunting's presence is half implied in Sinclair's acknowledgement of the 'wearied survivors of classical modernism', the editors of *Other* posit the 'discovery' of Basil Bunting at the age of 65 as 'lasting reproof to British literary circles' and point to his career as 'an exemplar for much of [their] collection'.[18] The question of Bunting is both charged and emblematic. The years of neglect can also be viewed as a form of independence, resilience and a refusal to compromise. Neglect from the mainstream allows the opening of less familiar doors and the editors of both *Other* and *Conductors of Chaos* delineate a compelling, half-hidden world of pamphlets, chapbooks, small presses, bookshops, groups and splinter groups, pub readings, with or without music, 'happenings', European and American sympathies, all charged with an experimental and/or improvisational underground exuberance, becoming at times both a 'secret religion' and a form of resistance. Bunting provided a vital link with the modernist generation, and his readings at the Morden Tower, where his youthful audience saw him as a kind of ancient mariner coming home with exotic tales, not only made the medieval tower in Newcastle an iconic space, but they also vitalized the performative aspects of poetry which has had various long-lasting effects. Bunting was unwavering in his belief that poetry needed to be heard and the notion of 'performance' can manifest itself in various ways – concrete poetry and the visual word, sound poetry, cabaret and burlesque as well as the kind of performance poetry promoted by Apples and Snakes.[19] If these examples are considered to be part of a more radical, multi-disciplinary tradition, the idea of the poet as a performer both on the page and off the page has become central to more 'mainstream' productions too. Accordingly, the editors of *The New Poetry* (1993), who acknowledge Alvarez's earlier anthology and who provide space for several of the poets who were later defined as the New Generation, reaffirm 'the art's significance as public utterance'.[20] The editors of *Voice Recognition*: *21 Poets for the 21st Century* (2009), whose very title foregrounds the notion of transmission, considers the way in which younger poets have 'an increased awareness of how to deliver a poem to an audience'.[21]

Bunting's outsider/insider status was not only symbolic. His resurrection, post-*Briggflatts*, made him a cultural agent naturally sympathetic to counter-cultural values. In 1971–2, 'as part of an organizational and political coup for a poetics of dissent and dislocation, Basil Bunting became President of the Poetry Society and Eric Mottram took over the editorship of the *Poetry Review* [the Society's house journal].'[22] The Poetry Society, funded by the Arts Council, had become a tired if venerable organization with typically conservative instincts. Mottram's dispensation heralded a furiously contested half decade that is revealing in a number of ways. By 1975, radical poets had taken most of the seats on the General Council and Mottram radicalized the journal, creating 'workshops, readings and experimental performances'[23] whose protagonists included Bob Cobbing, Cris Cheek and Lawrence Upton. Under Mottram's editorship, *The Poetry Review* opened its doors to American poets such as Charles Olson, Robert Creeley, George Oppen, Robert Duncan and Gary Snyder. Although this interregnum lasted only until 1977, by which time the conservatives had regrouped and the radicals resigned, the 'poetry wars' of the 1970s brought to the fore the antagonisms and ideological conflicts that stood behind 'officially sanctioned poetry' and experimental alternatives. Peter Barry discusses 'the Battle of Earls Court' in *Poetry Wars*. [24]

Bunting was now in his seventies and the guerrilla raids and in-fighting described above were being carried out by younger poets but it is interesting to see how this generation might choose to see the author of *Briggflatts* as a charismatic figurehead for a range of dissentient poetries. Bunting's experiences of prison, his animus towards Bloomsbury, his Nonconformist upbringing, his celebration of northern English culture far removed from the historical centre of power, his ability to survive as a poet outside the official channels of patronage, as well as his connections with the experimental dynamic of the early twentieth-century modernists, made him something of a talisman. Neither was he afraid to speak out in his newly acquired roles. Addressing the Northern Arts AGM in 1977, Bunting argued that 'a system that leaves many artists [...] as poor as some of them are after a life of putting up with poverty has something seriously wrong with it. It looks to me as though much of what the Arts Council does is mainly a way of evading its admittedly difficult task.'[25]

An assessment of the legacies of any poet is necessarily complicated. Roy Fisher considers the significance of the Northumbrian poet in a piece entitled 'Debt to Mr. Bunting'.[26] In any case, the Bunting of *Briggflatts* is quite different from the Bunting of the early Sonatas even if we recognize how the later poem responds to some of the questions being asked in the earlier work. Although one sees how in the 1960s and the 1970s Bunting had become either friend or source of inspiration to a diverse range of younger poets including Pickard, MacSweeney, Turnbull, Jonathan Williams, Fisher, and although one learns how his readings at both The Morden Tower and elsewhere became a talking point and that his lecturing stints in America inspired many including the American poet August Kleinzahler,[27] there has never been a 'Bunting School'. The singularity of Bunting's career, both within and outside the world of poetry, and his highly eclectic range of literary influences from Horace, Firdosi and others, Wyatt, Raleigh, Malherbe, Wordsworth through to Pound work against convenient labelling. How might the circle be squared, asks Richard Price, before conceding that a poet like Bunting 'need take no lessons in verse-rationalisation [...] Inconsistencies are the poet's riches not his debt'.[28] Bunting's legacies, in his various roles as technician, critic, translator, university lecturer, and 'Hemingwayan man of action', are both tangible and intangible.[29] Davie's championing of Bunting's deep-rooted 'Englishness' needs to be put alongside enthusiastic American responses. In part, this is a recognition of Bunting's relationship with Pound and Zukofsky and a sympathy on Bunting's part for the American line. Quartermain points out that it is difficult to remember 'how marginal (indeed how alien) to English readers, critics, and publishers American writers besides Eliot were; notice the history not only of Ezra Pound in Britain, satirized, lampooned, attacked, but of William Carlos Williams, who did not find an English publisher until he was dead.' Quartemain continues: 'It is extremely difficult to imagine the sort of perspicacity and courage it took for a young Englishman in the early 1920s to hitch his wagon to the stars of Pound and Eliot.'[30] Terrell's *Basil Bunting: Man and Poet* is a significant contribution to Bunting studies. This American enthusiasm also came out of the post-*Briggflatts* period in which the poet spent extended periods reading and lecturing in the United States. One might also note Bunting's interest in the work of the American poet Lorine Niedecker.

Bunting's markedly 'masculine' poetry with its 'modernist' vigour has meant that his work has been better received by male poets and critics. The Festschrift *Madeira and Toasts for Basil Bunting's 75th Birthday* serves up an impressive miscellany of tributes – poetic, critical and visual – from poets and critics such as Fisher, Morgan, Tomlinson, Raworth, MacDiarmid and Kenner, but it's an almost entirely male Festschrift.[31] The poet Elaine Randell argues that 'Bunting is a northern man's poet because that's how he's been seen by his followers. A male club I can't add justification for that but it's really how I feel.'[32] Maggie O'Sullivan maintains, on the other hand, that Bunting had had a strong influence on her work: 'I felt a strong affinity with his negotiation of sound-sense in language and concerns with place, "place" as sounded on the tongue as well as geographical environment [...] Bunting presented his work in a performative and extremely sonic textual demonstration off the page. There's a tremendous muscularity in his language.'[33]

Sister Victoria Forde, whose contribution to Bunting studies has been significant, argues that because Bunting lived during most of the twentieth century, his poetry 'provides a rich impression of his century' and that 'in a comparatively small output he compresses into honed lines a complex experience of its external and internal life.'[34] Although Bunting argued that 'the business of poetry is poetry and not social reform' (*M&P* 131), he has been effective in drawing our attention to the century's many episodes of 'penury/filth, disgust and fury' (*CP* 77). His poems, in a number of ways, describe economic burden, incarceration, torture, social injustice, the rhythms of urban life, military conflict, environmental crises and spiritual quest. 'The Complaint of the Morpethshire Farmer' (*CP* 114), for example, is a poignant poem about economic migration. According to Forde, 'From whatever perspective Basil Bunting's poetry is appreciated' his poetry 'provide[s] an overview of the twentieth century and stir[s] emotions more deeply than any merely statistical work could ever do.'[35]

The incidents of Bunting's biography amounted to, according to Corcoran, 'an oddly displaced life'.[36] Former inmate of Wormwood Scrubs, later squadron leader, British intelligence operative and vice-consul of Isfahan, Bunting's relationship with the Establishment was complicated. Similarly, his poetry creates a set of challenges for critics who like to compartmentalize. Although Davie posited Bunting as 'a card-carrying English Poundian' he did so in order to qualify the implications of that description. Davie has, in fact, determinedly placed the poet in a northern English context and has seen his relationship with Northumbria and the Quaker tradition as quintessential components of an internationalized *Englishness*. Having cited Bunting's ode 'On the Fly-Leaf of Pound's Cantos', Corcoran sees the third section of *Briggflatts*, in which the Northumbrian poet draws on Firdosi's account of Alexander's journey to the mountains of Gog and Magog, as 'an allegory of Bunting's wrestle with Pound as the unignorable and terrifying precursor'.[37] Bunting's 'release' from his modernist precursors – one who 'cribbed in a madhouse', one 'suffocated by adulation' (*CP* 55–6) – is ultimately sanctioned in the composition of *Briggflatts*.

Davie's negotiations with British and non-British poetries were variegated and inclusive. Much of the time he was seeking to bridge the perceived distance between modernist and English traditions, calling for 'an essay or a monograph that would map a way into the poetic universe of Pound by the firmly interlinked stages of an English route that runs from Landor to Hardy through Browning'.[38] In *Thomas Hardy and British Poetry*, Davie devotes chapters to both Larkin and J. H. Prynne, and although here in this study Larkin and Bunting have been presented as representatives of antithetical poetics, one might find some common ground in the way that both poets were instinctively anti-theoretical and saw the poem as an essentially pleasure-giving force. Davie challenges the received idea that Euro-American modernism irrevocably interrupted the English line. *Briggflatts* presented itself as an example of how internationalism need not be incompatible with a passionate localism. Bunting's engagement with modernist poetics did not prevent him from displaying a range of English, and Old English, linguistic reflexes, including the use of 'kennings' and a massy consonantal drive that draws attention to the 'materiality of the signifier'.[39] Bunting's historical consciousness is important too: 'the matter that Bunting packs into *Briggflatts*, the content of it, the experience that it re-creates and celebrates, is indelibly and specifically English enough to satisfy anybody.'[40]

Davie's *Under Briggflatts: A History of Poetry in Great Britain 1960–1988*, in which poets as diverse as MacDiarmid, Feinstein and Larkin are discussed, takes its place amongst twentieth-century anthologies and critical studies, including *The Penguin Book of Contemporary British Poetry* and Kenner's *A Sinking Island*, and attempts to show readers on both sides of the Atlantic that British poetry is not yet – *pace* Perloff – paralysed 'by the burdensome sense of tradition' and that furthermore an ability to see beyond the limitations of the Movement reveals a range of traditions including a sympathy for international modernism.[41] Davie's *Under Briggflatts* presents an argument constructed by a former Movement poet which seeks to widen the very franchise that Movement orthodoxies had curtailed. Its very title makes Bunting's 1960s poem into a rallying call for a poetry that looks beyond British shores yet which at the same time digs deep into local terrain. If Davie's 1970s claim that *Briggflatts* is 'where English poetry has got to' seems less convincing in the early years of the twenty-first century, one can see how its advocacy comes in part from out of the cultural politics of the 1970s. Postmodernism or post-postmodernism rather than retro-modernism would seem to more accurately describe the poetic operations of the Martian School of the 1970s and 1980s and the New Generation Poets of the 1990s. Yet one can see how Bunting gifted the critic with an English poem that reflected the heroic modernism of an earlier age and which showed a viable alternative to the domesticated ironies and circumscribed parochialism of Movement-driven poetry. It was a poem that heralded possibilities and, as such, remains a lodestar for poets who take an innovative approach to the poetic tradition. Bunting's evocation of the north-east also challenged homogeneous accounts of Englishness by celebrating diversity and difference on a number of levels.[42] *Briggflatts*, with its regional and international reflexes, lent its weight to the redefining of British cultural politics in the post-war period.

8

Conclusion

Briggflatts was Basil Bunting's defining triumph. Technical problems in the earlier sonatas were now resolved. After many years of 'sharp study and long toil' (*SV* 314), the poet produced a work of intricate patterning and sonic drive. His handling of the poetic line remains an enduring legacy. He created an economy of expression which not infrequently drew on alliterative rhythms and monosyllabic precision, creating an auditory effect which rewarded the ear in varying ways. This gives rise to a vigorous if melopoeic compression not without bardic possibilities. The success of *Briggflatts* in the mid-1960s gave energy to the British Poetry Revival, a period of poetic experiment that sought to transcend the narrowness of the Movement by re-examining modernist legacies on both sides of the Atlantic. *Briggflatts* heralded the 'discovery' of a poet who although steeped in international modernist traditions fashioned a profoundly English poem. There had been a long hiatus before the emergence of *Briggflatts*. Its success placed Bunting in the limelight and there would have been some expectation of future work. Apart from a handful of odes including '*At Briggflatts meetinghouse*' (*CP* 145) and '*Perche no Spero*' (*CP* 146), nothing of import materialized. The post-*Briggflatts* years were given over to intermittent periods of teaching, interviews and readings rather than further poetic production. This might seem like a lost opportunity but there were material reasons behind it. Makin argues that notwithstanding Bunting's new-found literary fame he never became 'bankable' and the drudgery continued even as he reached his later years. It wasn't the drudgery of a provincial newspaper but nevertheless Bunting continued to face an uncertain future as he struggled to support his family and himself. Although American university teaching posts were quite well paid they were temporary and non-renewable so that 'from 1966 until his death in 1985, Bunting was never at any time in command of an income that could be expected to last more than two years from the date of its inception' (*SV* 314). Neither patronage near to home nor the Gulbenkian Foundation delivered Bunting from these tribulations and one can see how this financially difficult situation might have interfered with further creativity. Writing to Jonathan Williams in 1973, Bunting points out that invitations from Cambridge University were frequent: 'Of course we cannot offer to pay a fee, but we will make sure you get a good meal' (*SV* 318). 'Poet appointed dare not decline/to walk among the bogus' begins the second section of *Briggflatts* and any account of Bunting needs to consider how, even post-*Briggflatts*, the poet largely functioned outside the official channels of patronage. Makin argues:

> It is impossible to know whether the material compulsions in his later years were as Bunting portrayed them; still less possible to know whether, had he been given a Guggenheim for life from the age of 65, he would have produced more than he did. What is certain is that, in so far as it is possible for a public and its institutions to place a writer in circumstances where he can write, our public and our institutions did almost nothing. The loss to Basil Bunting matters less than the loss to poetry, which is also ours. (*SV* 318)

There were, nevertheless, tantalising glimpses of a new unfinished work. Writing to Forde on 23 May 1972, after a long voyage from British Columbia, Bunting pointed out that a number of themes which he had been wrestling with over the last three years had begun to take shape.

> One night I saw the new moon, the very first new moon, emerging from the old moon as Helen, Selanna, the new moon, must have emerged from Leda's egg; and the next night I watched Jupiter as a drop of molten silver sliding down the flank of the new moon. As I turned away from this marvellous sight I caught a glimpse of a very young girl who seemed obviously the new moon in flesh, slim, graceful, blonde; and instantly many old themes began to assemble themselves as though this were the keystone enabling them to form an arch, themes of renewal, mainly, closely bound, though I had never perceived it. (*PBB* 243)

Subsequently, Bunting sent the first thirty lines of the 'New Moon' Sonata:

> Such syllables flicker out of grass:
> 'What beckons goes'; and no glide lasts
> nor wings are ever in even beat long.
> A male season with paeonies, birds bright under thorn.
> Light pelts hard now my sub's low.
> it carves my stone as hail mud
> till day's net drapes the haugh,
> glaze crackled by flung drops.
> What use? Elegant hope, fever of tune,
> new now, next, in the fall, to be dust.
>
> Wind shakes a blotch of sun,
> flatter and tattle willow and oak alike
> sly as a trout's shadow on gravel.
> Light stots from stone, sets ridge and kerf quick
> as a shot skims rust from steel. Men of the north
> subject to being beheaded and cannot avoid it
> of a race that is naturally given that way.
> 'Uber sophiae sugens' in hourless dark,
> their midnight shimmers like noon.
> They clasp that axle fast.
>
> Those who lie with Loki's daughter,
> jawbones laid to her stiff cheek,
> hear rocks stir above the goaf;
> but a land swaddled in light? Listen, make out
> lightfall singing on a wall mottled grey
> and the wall growls, tossing light,
> prow in tide, boulder in a foss,
> A man shrivels in many days, eyes thirst for night
> to scour and shammy the sky
> thick with dust and breath.

(PBB 243–4)

These lines, from any perspective, are charged with virtuosity. The monosyllabic and alliterative pressure along with the use of technical and dialect language are in the Bunting style: 'Light stots from stone, sets ridge and kerf quick/as shot skims rust from steel. Men of the north/subject to being beheaded and cannot avoid it'. If 'Starlight quivers' at the end of *Briggflatts*, this later piece also catches the light within the 'hourless dark' and as we saw at the end of *The Well*, where the River Styx is 'silvered by a wind from heaven', Bunting succeeds in retrieving a note of consolation even as the death rattle is sounded. There's a hint of Pound's mystical poetic of light – where in the 'light of light is the virtù' – even as the English poet moves away from Classical into Norse mythology. 'Those who lie with Loki's daughter' [the goddess of death] would seem to echo 'He lies with one to long for another', thus reworking the formula of mortality, creativity and sexual appetite. The 'New Moon' Sonata seems to be following *Briggflatts* in resisting eschatological certainties and light/dark, life/death binaries. This unfinished work would appear to be speculating on preternatural models of resurrection.

Bunting's Chomei 'clacked a few prayers' and this conclusion to the 'Japanese' poem might serve as a way of considering Bunting's legacies in general. If the earlier sonatas are fragmentary and sometimes vituperative, *Chomei* strikes a note of quietude and/or resignation and both *The Spoils* and *Briggflatts* are underpinned by spiritual quest. Poetry as prayer is rooted in the Christian tradition and we shouldn't be surprised that a poet schooled in the Quaker faith had an intrinsic sense of the sacred. Makin argues that silence was important to a number of religious figures 'whom Bunting would have acknowledged as forbears: from the continental Quietists who influenced later Quakerism [...] back to St. Francis and to all the Celtic-Northumbrian saints' (*SV* 206). Silence, in other words, becomes a poetic strategy in its own right. Bunting's poems are rarely exhortatory or didactic and the Coda to *Briggflatts* celebrates a kind of resonant 'negative capability', or a willingness to accept the limits of knowledge. In fact, the silent years before and after *Briggflatts* could be said to frame the spirituality intrinsic to the poem itself. If *Briggflatts* helped to radicalize the landscape of British poetry in the 1960s and 1970s – triggering Davie's claim that this 'is where English poetry has got to' – we have acknowledged that it would be difficult to argue so in the later years of the twentieth century or the early years of the twenty-first. Bunting's legacy may be thought to have an unknown quality; in any case legacies typically have a protean dynamic. The weighting of *Briggflatts* in the poet's oeuvre risks dwarfing the oeuvre as a whole and, in the wider scheme, Bunting's negotiations with modernist poetics hints at a chapter of British poetry that is still contested and only half-written. Caddel qualifies the usual notion that Bunting has had no direct 'heirs' by arguing that his poetic of innovation and discovery has 'inspired a great number of emerging British and American poets over the last few decades' (*CP* 13). Barry argues that the vitriol of earlier debates between conservatives and radicals has been superseded by a 'post-dualist' accommodation in that 'there is a widespread pre-occupation by poets of *all* persuasions today with more or less "experimental" explorations of such things as: linguistic registers, implied voices, varieties of narrative technique and viewpoint, ways of using metaphor to undermine the "real", and various ways of using myth.'[1] A similar point is made in the introduction to *The Salt Book of Younger Poets*.[2] Quartermain maintains that whereas Eliot 'carefully inscribed himself into the tradition moulded on works imported from other lands, a tradition central, monolithic, and possessed of power', Bunting bequeathed a set of radical strategies insofar as the North-umbrian poet 'problematises that tradition, problematises the dominant ideology, problematises the hegemony of English Letters, by asserting the primacy of sound over meaning'.[3]

The editors of *Voice Recognition*, an anthology for the beginning of the twenty-first century, consider the importance of poetry as a performative art. They draw our attention to young poets who write about a damaged environment and, acknowledging the importance of travel and translation, they argue that 'leading new poets should represent progress, daring, originality and (where possible) an extension of the poetic tradition.' In fact, they celebrate the fact that 'there are meaningful explorations of relationships between page and performance, modernist and post-modern, experimental and avant-garde.'[4] By this reckoning, one might claim that some of Bunting's notions have been passed down to the 'unabashed boys and girls' of a later generation and that in some respects Bunting stands as an unannounced tutelary figure behind this recent anthology. He would have been particularly interested in Toby Martinez de las Rivas (b. 1978) who moved to the North-East to study history and archaeology at the University of Durham. The poet cites the landscape of Northumberland and the work of Barry MacSweeney as key influences.[5]

121

Bunting suggested that his epitaph might read 'A minor poet not conspicuously dishonest'. It is a modest assertion and this study, variously, has sought to evaluate the ways in which his relatively small oeuvre has had a powerful impact and ensured a critical re-evaluation of British poetry in the post-war period. Bunting's life and work stand outside easy description and his followers have tended to be passionate advocates. The history of *Briggflatts*, in terms of its composition and sudden emergence in the 1960s, enjoys a somewhat miraculous dimension. Rather like a comet in the sky, the poem created a sense of wonder which has, in turn, fashioned a mythology of its own. Although the work constituted an endpoint for the poet rather than a new beginning – 'The star you steer by is gone' – its music continues to reverberate and excite. August Kleinzahler, studying under Bunting at the University of Victoria in British Columbia in 1971–2, once asked the English poet whether 'it bugged him that he wasn't famous like Ted Hughes or Robert Lowell'. Bunting 'answered easily and with equanimity, "No, not really, I'll be read long after I'm gone."'[6]

Notes

CHAPTER 1. INTRODUCTION

1. See Bunting's *Selected Poems: Ford Madox Ford* (Cambridge, Mass.: Pym-Randall Press 1971).
2. See *Basil Bunting on Poetry* ed. Peter Makin (Baltimore: Johns Hopkins University Press, 1999).
3. See 'Basil Bunting's Emigrant Ballads' in Peter Robinson's *Twentieth Century Poetry: Selves and Situations* (Oxford: Oxford University Press, 2003), 39–48. Bunting edited Joseph Skipsey's *Selected Poems* (Sunderland: Ceolfrith Press, 1976). Skipsey was a self-educated 'Pitman Poet' (1832–1903) who began his working life at the age of seven and who helped document the hardships of nineteenth-century miners, often employing balladic form.
4. Keith Tuma, *Fishing By Obstinate Isles: Modern and Postmodern British Poetry and American Readers* (Evanston, Ill.: Northwestern University Press, 1998), 52.
5. Blake Morrison and Andrew Motion (eds.), *The Penguin Book of Contemporary British Verse* (London: Penguin, 1982), 11.
6. See *Conductors of Chaos* (London: Picador, 1996) whose editor Ian Sinclair provides a feisty argument in favour of poetic traditions that fall outside a hedged-in middle ground driven by the Movement and its successors. Philip Larkin was the leading exponent of the Movement.
7. Hugh Kenner, *A Sinking Island: The Modern English Writers* (London: Barrie and Jenkins, 1988), 7. The book is dedicated to Bunting.
8. Peter Quartermain, *Basil Bunting: Poet of the North* (Durham: Basil Bunting Poetry Centre, 1990), 8.
9. Richard Caddel (ed.), *Sharp Study and Long Toil: Basil Bunting Special Issue* (Durham: A Durham University Journal in association with Basil Bunting Poetry Centre, 1995), 99.
10. James McGonigal and Richard Price (eds.), *The Star You Steer By: Basil Bunting and British Modernism* (Amsterdam: Rodopi, 2000), 14.

CHAPTER 2. A POET'S LIFE

1. Richard Caddel and Anthony Flowers, *Basil Bunting: A Northern Life* (Durham: Newcastle Libraries and Information Service in association with the Basil Bunting Poetry Centre, 1997), 9.
2. Peter Quartermain, *Basil Bunting: Poet of the North* (Durham: Basil Bunting Poetry Centre, 1990), 6.
3. 'I Remember, I Remember', *Collected Poems* (London: Faber and Faber, 1988), 81.
4. 'An Interview with the *Observer*', *Required Writing: Miscellaneous Pieces 1955–1982* (London: Faber and Faber, 1983), 54.
5. William Carlos Williams argued that 'The only universal is the local as savages, artist and – to a lesser extent – peasants know', *William Carlos Williams: Selected Poems* ed. Charles Tomlinson (Harmondsworth: Penguin, 1976), 11.
6. In *The Poetic Achievements of Donald Davie and Charles Tomlinson: Expanding Vision, Voice, and Rhythm in Late Twentieth-Century English Poetry* (Lewiston, NY: The Edwin Mellen Press, 2010), I consider the ways in which Tomlinson, in particular, pursues a poetic of factuality, rooted in place, which nods at moments to Bunting's poetic.
7. Peter Burger, *Theory of the Avant-Garde* (1984) trans. Michael Shaw (Minneapolis, Minn.: University of Minnesota Press) cited in Rebecca Beasley, *Theorists of Modernist Poetry: T. S. Eliot, T. E. Hulme, Ezra Pound* (London and New York: Routledge, 2007), 119.
8. A quick roll-call would include, amongst others, Pound and Zukofsky, Yeats, Eliot, Ford Madox Ford, David Jones, MacDiarmid, Mina Loy and Lorine Niedecker.
9. Canto LXXIV, *The Cantos* (London: Faber and Faber, 1994), 445.
10. John Tytell, *Ezra Pound: The Solitary Volcano* (London: Bloomsbury, 1987), 319.
11. *Tigullio Itineraries: Ezra Pound and Friends* from 'Ezra Pound, Language and Persona' ed. Massimo Bacigalupo and William Pratt, *Quaderni di Palazzo Serra 15* (Rapallo: Università degli Studi di Genova, 2005), 380.
12. Dale Reagan, 'An Interview with Basil Bunting', *Montemora 3* (Spring 1977), 72.
13. 'They Say Etna' (*CP* 182) is brimming with political vitriol.
14. Richard Caddel (ed.), *Sharp Study and Long Toil: Basil Bunting Special Issue* (Durham: A Durham University Journal in association with the Basil Bunting Poetry Centre, 1995), 93–4.
15. The relationship between Yeats and Pound was cemented by personal factors. Pound married Dorothy Shakespear whose

mother Olivia had had a relationship with Yeats after they had met at a *Yellow Book* dinner in 1894.

16. Michael Alexander and James McGonigal (eds.), *Sons of Ezra: British Poets and Ezra Pound* (Amsterdam: Rodopi, 1995), 121.

17. One might have bumped into more than one Nobel Prize winner on the *lungomare*. Gerhardt Hauptmann, the German playwright was also part of the Rapallo group. A newspaper cutting, kept by Bunting's daughter Bourtai, dated January 1932, declares 'Prominent Literati Arriving at Rapallo To Pass Winter Season' (*PBB* 32). It refers to Hauptmann, Pound, William B. Yeats, Max Beerbohm and 'the poet Basil Bunting' who 'is rejoicing in the arrival of a baby daughter born in the Protestant hospital at Genoa'.

18. In November 1931 it was announced by *Poetry* that *Villon* had been awarded the annual Lyric Prize of $50.

19. Local talent included the violinist Olga Rudge and the pianist Gerhart Münch; music included that of Scriabin, Stravinsky and Satie.

20. *Il Mare: Supplemento Letterario* ed. Società Letteraria Rapallo (Rapallo: Commune di Rapallo, 1999).

21. William Carlos Williams, *The Autobiography of William Carlos Williams* (New York: Random House, 1951), 264.

22. Caddel and Flowers, *Basil Bunting: A Northern Life*, 39.

23. 'Statement', *Required Writing: Miscellaneous Pieces 1955–1982* (London: Faber and Faber, 1983), 79.

24. Kingsley Amis, *Poets of the 1950s* ed. D. J. Enright (Tokyo: The Keneyusha Press, 1955).

25. Robert Conquest (ed.) *New Lines* (London: Macmillan, 1956), xi.

26. There's a fascinating account of this first encounter written by Pickard entitled 'Serving My Time to a Trade' in *Paideuma*, 9/1 (Spring 1980), 155–63.

27. Alexander and McGonigal (eds.), *Sons of Ezra: British Poets and Ezra Pound*, 121.

CHAPTER 3. THE EARLY SONATAS: *VILLON, ATTIS: OR, SOMETHING MISSING, THE WELL OF LYCOPOLIS, AUS DEM ZWEITEN REICH*

1. *Il Mare: Supplemento Letterario 1932–1933*, ed. Literary Society of Rapallo (Rapallo: Commune di Rapallo, 1999), 72–3.

2. The anti-Romantic formula of 'impersonality' is posited and expounded upon in T. S. Eliot's all-important essay 'Tradition and the Individual Talent' in *The Sacred Wood: Essays on Poetry and*

Criticism (London: Faber and Faber, 1997). See pages 39–49.

3. Michael Hamburger, *The Truth of Poetry: Tensions in Modern Poetry from Baudelaire to the 1960s* (London: Weidenfeld and Nicolson, 1969), 122.

4. Ibid. 122–3.

5. Louis Zukofsky in the Preface to *A Test of Poetry*, 1948 (Middletown, Conn.: Wesleyan University Press, 2000).

6. Peter Quartermain, *Basil Bunting: Poet of the North* (Durham: Basil Bunting Poetry Centre, 1990), 15.

7. Eric Mottram, 'Conversation with Basil Bunting on the Occasion of his 75th Birthday', *Poetry Information* 19 (Autumn 1978), 5.

8. *François Villon: Selected Poems*, trans. Peter Dale (London: Penguin, 1988), 10.

9. *The Complete Works of François Villon*, trans. Anthony Bonner with an introduction by William Carlos Williams (New York: Bantam Books, 1960), xxii.

10. Ibid. xxiii.

11. Kenneth Cox, 'A Commentary on Basil Bunting's *Villon*', *Agenda*, 16/1 (Spring 1978), 20.

12. Ibid.

13. Richard Caddel and Anthony Flowers, *Basil Bunting: A Northern Life* (Durham: Newcastle Libraries and Information Service in association with Basil Bunting Poetry Centre, 1997), 49.

14. Clément Marot (1496–1544) was a French poet of the Renaissance period whose work bridged the medieval period and the classicizing poets of *La Pléiade*. Marot edited and published the work of Villon.

15. At the end of *Articulate Energy: An Inquiry Into the Syntax of English Poetry* Davie argues that 'For poetry to be great it must reek of the human, as Wordsworth's poetry does'; Donald Davie, *Purity of Diction in English Verse and Articulate Energy* (Manchester: Carcanet, 2006), 354.

16. Cox, 'A Commentary on Basil Bunting's *Villon*', 24.

17. Eliot, 'Tradition and the Individual Talent', 40–1.

18. Cox, 'A Commentary on Basil Bunting's *Villon*', 32.

17. Anthony Suter, 'Time and the Literary Past in the Poetry of Basil Bunting', *Contemporary Literature*, 12/4 (Autumn 1971), 524.

20. From *François Villon: Selected Poems*, 65. Dale translates:

> I know that rich or poor, the wise
> or foolish, parishioner or priest,
> nobles or peasants, prince and miser,
> high or low, beauty or beast,
> ladies in high-turned collars, least
> and last whatever their conception,

high hat or headscarf, west or east –
Death seizes all without exception. (Le Testamant, stanza 39)

21. *The Consolation of Philosophy* was written by Boethius (*c.*524) whilst in prison awaiting trial and subsequent execution. This makes the work a supreme example of Prison Literature and it became hugely important to later medieval writers and scholars. Lady Philosophy consoles Boethius by reminding him of the transitory nature of wealth and fame.

22. In *Poetry* (March 1913) we find several emphatic statements regarding imagism from F. S. Flint and Ezra Pound which include 'Direct treatment of the "thing" whether subjective or objective' and 'Use no superfluous word, no adjective which does not reveal something...' and, of huge significance, 'Go in fear of abstractions...', *Imagist Poetry* ed. Peter Jones (London: Penguin Books, 1985), 18–19.

23. See Donald Davie, *Ezra Pound: Poet as Sculptor* (New York: Oxford University Press, 1964); in this important contribution to Poundian studies, Davie argues a natural and illustrative connection between the art of sculpture and Poundian-modernist poetics.

24. Cox, 'A Commentary on Basil Bunting's *Villon*', 35.

25. *Selected Prose of T. S. Eliot* ed. Frank Kermode (London: Faber, 1975), 177–8.

26. Neil Corcoran, *English Poetry Since 1940* (London and New York: Longman, 1993), 3.

27. Cited in 'Modern Poetry' by James Longenbach in *The Cambridge Companion to Modernism* ed. Michael Levenson (Cambridge: Cambridge University Press, 1999), 100.

28. Richard Caddel (ed.), *Sharp Study and Long Toil: Basil Bunting Special Issue* (Durham: Durham University Journal in association with Basil Bunting Poetry Centre, 1995), 109.

29. In earlier versions Cybele falls in love with Attis, a young shepherd who is subject to a vow of chastity. When he breaks his vow Cybele strikes him with a frenzied delirium in the course of which he mutilates himself. When he recovers from his madness he is on the point of suicide when Cybele turns him into a fir-tree.

30. 'Reader, imagine! I grew faint at heart,/to hear these cursed phrases ringing out./I truly thought I'd never make it back.' in Dante's *Inferno*, trans. Robin Kirkpatrick (London: Penguin Classics, 2006), Canto 8, lines 94–7, 69.

31. 'The colour that failing courage brought out/so quickly in me', ibid. Canto 9, lines 1–2, 73.

32. James McGonigal and Richard Price (eds.), *The Star You Steer By: Basil Bunting and British Modernism*, 111.

33. In *The Anxiety of Influence: A Theory of Poetry*, Harold Bloom

announces that his concern 'is only with strong poets, major figures with the persistence to wrestle with their strong precursors, even to the death' (London: Oxford University Press, 1975), 5.

34. Caddel (ed.), *Sharp Study and Long Toil: Basil Bunting Special Issue*, 107.
35. James McGonigal and Richard Price (eds.), *The Star You Steer By: Basil Bunting and British Modernism* (Amsterdam: Rodopi, 2000), 11.
36. This is Horace's phrase from *Odes*, 2.5, which refers to Gyges 'whom, if you put him in a group of girls, the sharpest-witted strangers would fail to make out the difference, hidden by his unbound hair and his girl-boy face'.
37. Dale Reagan, 'An Interview with Basil Bunting' Montemora, 3 (Spring 1977), 75.
38. Quartermain, *Basil Bunting: Poet of the North*, 12.
39. Caddel (ed.), *Sharp Study and Long Toil: Basil Bunting Special Issue*, 101.
40. Anthony Suter, 'The Writer in the Mirror. Basil Bunting and T. S. Eliot: Parody and Parallel', *Paideuma* 9/1 (Spring 1980), 94.

CHAPTER 4. *CHOMEI AT TOYAMA* AND *THE SPOILS*

1. Anthony Suter, 'Time and the Literary Past in the Poetry of Basil Bunting', *Contemporary Literature* 12/4 (Autumn 1991), 522.
2. Matsuo Basho, 'Knapsack Notebook' (Oi No Kobumi), trans. David Landis Barnhill in *Basho's Journey: The Literary Prose of Matsuo Basho* (Albany, NY: Suny Press; 2005), 30.
3. The definition is found in Pound's *ABC of Reading* (London: Faber and Faber, 1991), 92 ; the story goes that Bunting handed Pound a German/Italian dictionary which translated Dichten as Condensare which became, in turn, a useful shorthand for both men's poetic practice.
4. Donald Keene (ed.), *Anthology of Japanese Literature from the Earliest Era to the Mid-Nineteenth Century* (New York: UNESCO, 1955), 197–8.
5. Peter Makin (ed.),*Basil Bunting on Poetry* (Baltimore: Johns Hopkins University Press, 1999), 128.
6. Kenneth White, *Open World: The Collected Poems 1960–2000* (Edinburgh: Polygon Books, 2003), 614.
7. Kenneth Cox, 'The Aesthetic of Basil Bunting', *Agenda*, 4/3 (Autumn 1966), 27.
8. James McGonigal and Richard Price (eds.), *The Star You Steer By: Basil Bunting and British Modernism*, (Amsterdam: Rodopi, 2000), 250.
9. See Psalm 91.3: 'For he will deliver you from the snare of the fowler'.

CHAPTER 5. ODES AND OVERDRAFTS

1. Keith Tuma, *Fishing By Obstinate Isles: Modern and Postmodern British Poetry and American Readers* (Evanston, Ill.: Northwestern University Press, 1998), 169–70.
2. Jean-Michel Rabaté, *1913: The Cradle of Modernism* (Oxford: Blackwell Publishing, 2007), 23–4.
3. R. S. Woof, 'Basil Bunting's Poetry' *Stand*, 8/2 (1966), 28.
4. Guido Cavalcanti (c.1255–1300), was a major Florentine poet, generally credited with creating the *dolce stil nuovo* ('The Sweet New Style'). He was a contemporary of Dante and of much interest to both Eliot and Pound.
5. In a poignant and telling letter written from Fox Cottage, Hexham on 20 March 1985, a few weeks before his death, Bunting wrote to Massimo Bacigalupo, Poundian critic at the University of Genoa. He apologizes for not having written for a long time, blaming his '85 years'. He continues: 'The same years prohibit me from travelling. Old men are disgusting to themselves as well as those who try to put up with them. I shall not revisit Italy, probably not even London.' He signs off: 'Snow and cold winds still imprison me. I survive with whisky's help. Auguri.'
6. Peter Robinson, *Poetry and Translation: The Art of the Impossible* (Liverpool: Liverpool University Press, 2001) 11–12.
7. Donald Davie, *The Poet in the Imaginary Museum: Essays of Two Decades* ed. Barry Alpert (Manchester: Carcanet, 1977), 155.
8. Ibid. 157.
9. James McGonigal and Richard Price (eds.), *The Star You Steer By: Basil Bunting and British Modernism* (Amsterdam: Rodopi, 2000), 97.
10. Dale Reagan, 'An Interview with Basil Bunting', *Montemora*, 3 (Spring, 1977), 73.
11. Ibid. 69–70.
12. McGonigal and Price (eds.), *The Star You Steer By*, 203.
13. G. M. Wickens, 'The Persian Conception of Artistic Unity in Poetry and its Implications in Other Fields', *Bulletin of the School of Oriental and African Studies*, XIV (1952), 704–5.
14. McGonigal and Price (eds.), *The Star You Steer By*, 201.

CHAPTER 6. *BRIGGFLATTS*

1. Gary Day and Brian Docherty (eds.), *British Poetry from the 1950s to the 1990s: Politics and Art* (London: Macmillan, 1997), 27.
2. In an interesting analysis of the American explorer and travel writer

Corporal John Ledyard (1751–88), Donald Davie in 'John Ledyard: The American Traveller and his Sentimental Journeys' from *Older Masters: Essays and Reflections on English and American Literature* (Manchester: Carcanet, 1992), 212–13, cites a letter from the American which claims that 'to be travelling is to be in error'. Davie continues by arguing that 'Ledyard is teasing out the puns which link "error" through "errant" with "wandering" and that the landscape through which he errs is [...] the epistemological landscape through which one seeks knowledge and self-knowledge.'

3. Michael Schmidt, *Reading Modern Poetry* (London: Routledge, 1989), 39.
4. Michael Alexander and James McGonigal (eds.), *Sons of Ezra: British Poets and Ezra Pound* (Amsterdam: Rodopi, 1995), 121.
5. Ibid. 124.
6. Edwad Lucie-Smith, *Contemporary Poets of the English Language* (London: Saint James Press, 1970), 162.
7. Charles Tomlinson, 'The Return', *New Collected Poems* (Manchester: Carcanet/Oxford Poets, 2009), 414.
8. Donald Davie, *Six Epistles to Eva Hesse* from *Collected Poems* (Manchester: Carcanet, 2002), 273.
9. Donald Davie, *Under Briggflatts: A History of Poetry in Great Britain 1960–1988* (Manchester: Carcanet, 1989), 41.
10. Brigflatts the place is spelt with one 'g', unlike the poem.
11. Michael Hamburger, *The Truth of Poetry: Tensions in Modern Poetry from Baudelaire to the 1960s* (London: Weidenfeld and Nicolson, 1969), 273.
12. Thom Gunn, 'What the Slowworm Said', *PN Review* 27, 7/1 (1982), 29.
13. Ezra Pound, 'Credo', *Ezra Pound: Selected Prose 1909–1965* ed. William Cookson (London: Faber and Faber, 1973), 53.
14. Jonathan Bate, *The Song of the Earth* (London: Picador, 2000), 234.
15. R. S. Woof, 'Basil Bunting's Poetry' *Stand*, 8/2 (1966), 30.
16. Timothy Clark, *Charles Tomlinson* (Tavistock: Northcote House Publishers: Writers and Their Work, 1999). In this study of Charles Tomlinson, an English poet with internationalist persuasions, Clark argues that Tomlinson's attachment to place is not dissimilar to Bunting's engagement with Northumbria, as well as David Jones' relationship with Wales and Hugh MacDiarmid's attachment to Scotland, p. 9.
17. Massimo Bacigalupo, 'Scrittori Anglofoni in Liguria nel Novecento', *Bilancio della Letteratura del Novecento in Liguria* ed. Giovanni Ponte (Genoa: Academia Ligure di Scienze e Lettere, 2000), 214.
18. Peter Quartermain and Warren Tallman, 'Basil Bunting Talks about

Briggflatts', *Georgia Straight Writing Supplement*, 6 (1970), n.p.

19. P. Johnstone, '[Two Interviews]'. *Meantime*, 1 (1977), 74.

20. Gary Day and Brian Docherty (eds.), *British Poetry from the 1950s to the 1990s: Politics and Art*, 28.

21. Ibid. 27.

22. Peter Makin (ed.), *Basil Bunting on Poetry* (Baltimore: Johns Hopkins University Press, 1999), 1–18.

23. Eric Mottram, 'Conversation with Basil Bunting on the Occasion of his 75th Birthday', *Poetry Information*, 19 (Autumn 1978), Basil Bunting Special Issue.

24. Makin (ed.), *Basil Bunting on Poetry*, 170.

25. Mottram, 'Conversation with Basil Bunting on the Occasion of his 75th Birthday', 7.

26. Makin (ed.), *Basil Bunting on Poetry*, 3.

27. Day and Docherty (eds.), *British Poetry from the 1950s to the 1990s* , 26.

28. Davie, *Under Briggflatts*, 42.

29. Don Share, 'Short Notes on a Longish Poem', *Basil Bunting: Briggflatts* (Northumberland: Bloodaxe, 2009), 76.

30. Day and Docherty (eds.), *British Poetry from the 1950s to the 1990s*, 23.

31. Ibid. 25.

32. There has been some commentary on the range of Bunting's pronunciation. If Throckley was his linguistic alma mater he was of course quite able to put on his wing-commander's voice when necessary.

33. Davie, *Under Briggflatts*, 40.

34. Richard Caddel and Anthony Flower (eds.), *Basil Bunting: A Northern Life* (Durham: Newcastle Libraries and Information Service in association with Basil Bunting Poetry Centre, 1997), 33–5.

35. Gunn, 'What the Slowworm Said', 29.

36. Bate, *The Song of the Earth*, 235.

37. Richard Caddel (ed.), *Sharp Study and Long Toil: Basil Bunting Special Issue* (Durham: Durham University Journal in association with Basil Bunting Poetry Centre, 1995), 90.

38. Bate, *The Song of the Earth*, 235.

39. Alexander and McGonigal (eds.), *Sons of Ezra*, 131.

40. Bate, *The Song of the Earth*, 231.

41. Peter Quartermain, *Basil Bunting: Poet of the North* (Durham: Basil Bunting Poetry Centre, 1990), 10.

42. Tony Lopez, 'Under Saxon the Stone: National Identity in Basil Bunting's *Briggflatts'*, in Caddel (ed.), *Sharp Study and Long Toil*, 114.

43. Makin (ed.), *Basil Bunting on Poetry*, 16.

44. Quartermain, *Basil Bunting: Poet of the North*, 9.

45. Davie, *Under Briggflatts*, 39.

46. Ibid. 38–9.

47. Alexander and McGonigal (eds.), *Sons of Ezra*, 131.

CHAPTER 7. CRITICAL PERSPECTIVES

1. Donald Davie, *The Poet in the Imaginary Museum: Essays of Two Decades* (Manchester: Carcanet, 1977), 292.
2. D. J. Enright (ed.), *Poets of the 1950s: An Anthology of New English Verse* (Tokyo: Kenkyusha, 1955), 47.
3. Davie, *The Poet in the Imaginary Museum*, 74.
4. Ibid. 48.
5. Ibid. 67.
6. Ibid. 32–42. 'T.S. Eliot: The End of An Era'.
7. William Carlos Williams, *The Autobiography of William Carlos Williams* (New York: Random House, 1951), 174.
8. Richard Caddel (ed.), *Sharp Study and Long Toil: Basil Bunting Special Issue*, (Durham: Durham University Journal in association with Basil Bunting Poetry Centre, 1995), 101.
9. Davie, *The Poet in the Imaginary Museum*, 287.
10. Philip Larkin, *All What Jazz: A Record Diary 1961–71* (London: Faber, 1970), 17.
11. A full and useful account is found in Blake Morrison's *The Movement: English Poetry and Fiction of the 1950s* (Oxford: Oxford University Press, 1980). See also Zachary Leader (ed.), *The Movement Reconsidered: Essays on Larkin, Amis, Gunn, Davie and Their Contemporaries* (Oxford: Oxford University Press, 2009).
12. A. Alvarez (ed.), *The New Poetry* (London: Penguin, 1962), 21–32.
13. Peter Forbes, 'Talking about the New Generation', *Poetry Review* 84/1 (Spring 1994), 4.
14. Ian Sinclair (ed.), *Conductors of Chaos: A Poetry Anthology* (London: Picador, 1996), xiii–xx.
15. Keith Tuma, *Fishing By Obstinate Isles: Modern and Postmodern British Poetry and American Readers* (Evanston, Ill.: Northwestern University Press, 1998), 1.
16. Richard Caddel and Peter Quartemain (eds.), *Other: British and Irish Poetry Since 1970* (Hanover and London: Wesleyan University Press, 1999), xxii.
17. Ibid. xviii.
18. Ibid. xvi.
19. http://www.applesandsnakes.org/page/8/About+us (Accessed 6 April, 2012).
20. Michael Hulse, David Kennedy and David Morley (eds.), *The New Poetry* (Northumberland: Bloodaxe, 1993), 16.
21. James Byrne and Clare Pollard (eds.), *Voice Recognition: 21 Poets for*

the 21st Century (Northumberland: Bloodaxe), 14.

22. Caddel and Quartermain (eds.), *Other: British and Irish Poetry Since 1970*, xxiv.
23. Ibid.
24. Peter Barry, *Poetry Wars: British Poetry of the 1970s and the Battle of Earls Court* (Cambridge: Salt Publishing, 2006).
25. James McGonigal and Richard Price (eds.), *The Star You Steer By: Basil Bunting and British Modernism* (Amsterdam: Rodopi, 2000), 107.
26. Ibid. 11–16,
27. See August Kleinzahler's 'Remembering Bunting', *Scripsi*, 3/2–3 (August 1985), 8–9. Kleinzahler provides a fond description which comes from the American's 'great good fortune to study and spend time with Mr. Bunting at the University of Victoria in British Columbia' in 1971–2. Kleinzahler writes; 'he wasn't a man comfortable in an academic setting, and he was treated abominably by the creative writing faculty, who were jealous of him as only provincial hacks can be of a distinguished outlander they can't fathom', yet Kleinzahler thought Bunting 'a wonderful man, quite apart form his poetry, however diligently he tried to play the curmudgeon'.
28. McGonigal and Price (eds.), *The Star You Steer By*, 89.
29. Peter Makin (ed.), *Basil Bunting on Poetry* (Baltimore: Johns Hopkins University Press, 1999), xvi.
30. Peter Quartermain, *Basil Bunting: Poet of the North* (Durham: Basil Bunting Poetry Centre, 1990), 9.
31. It's worth noting Constance Pickard's birthday poem in which she writes 'He's very salty @ he/Takes us all with a pinch of it./I like him very much.' No page numbers.
32. McGonigal and Price (eds.), *The Star You Steer by*, 141.
33. Ibid. 135.
34. Ibid. 235.
35. Ibid. 250.
36. Neil Corcoran, *English Poetry Since 1940* (London and New York: Longman, 1993), 35.
37. Ibid. 28.
38. Donald Davie, *Thomas Hardy and British Poetry* (London: Routledge and Kegan Paul, 1973), 3.
39. Corcoran, *English Poetry Since 1940*, 29.
40. Davie, *The Poet in the Imaginary Museum*, 291.
41. Marjorie Perloff, 'The Two Poetries: An Introduction', *Contemporary Literature*, 18 (Summer 1977), 264.42.
42. See Sean O'Brien's 'As Deep as England' in *Poetry Review*, 102/1 (Spring 2012), 53–69. Although Bunting isn't mentioned the essay is both germane and useful.

CHAPTER 8. CONCLUSION

1. Peter Barry, *Poetry Wars: British Poetry of the 1970s and the Battle of Earls Court*, (Cambridge, Salt Publishing, 2006), 179.
2. Roddy Lumsden and Eloise Stonborough (eds.), *The Salt Book of Younger Poets* (London: Salt Publishing, 2011), xvi.
3. Peter Quartermain, *Basil Bunting: Poet of the North* (Durham: Basil Bunting Poetry Centre, 1990), 8.
4. James Byrne and Clare Pollard (eds.), *Voice Recognition: 21 Poets for the 21st Century* (Northumberland: Bloodaxe, 2009), 13.
5. Ibid. 86.
6. August Kleinzahler, 'Remembering Bunting', *Scripsi*, 3/2–3 (August 1985), 8.

Select Bibliography

MAJOR WORKS (POETRY) BY BASIL BUNTING

Redimiculum Matellarum, privately printed (Milan: Grafica Moderna, 1930).

Poems: 1950 (Galveston, Tex., The Cleaner's Press, 1950).

The Spoils (Newcastle upon Tyne: The Morden Tower Book Room, 1965).

First Book of Odes (London: Fulcrum Press, 1965).

Loquitur (London: Fulcrum Press, 1965).

Briggflatts (London: Fulcrum Press, 1966).

Briggflatts (*Poetry* 107/4, Jan. 1966).

Collected Poems (London: Fulcrum Press, 1968).

Collected Poems (Oxford: Oxford University Press, 1978).

The Complete Poems (Oxford: Oxford University Press, 1994).

Complete Poems (Newcastle upon Tyne: Bloodaxe, 2000). With an introduction by the Bunting scholar Richard Caddel, *Complete Poems* tweaks 'into place some errors' from *The Complete Poems* (OUP, 1994). Page references in the present study refer to this publication.

(ed.), *Selected Poems: Ford Madox Ford* (Cambridge, Mass.: Pym-Randall Press, 1971).

(ed.), *Joseph Skipsey: Selected Poems* (Sunderland: Coelfrith Press, 1976).

RECORDINGS

Swigg, Richard, (ed.), *The Recordings of Basil Bunting,* 8 cassettes issued by Keele University in association with the Basil Bunting Poetry Centre at Durham University, 1994. This recording was subsequently used on the double-cassette issued by Bloodaxe in 2000 and again in CD format in *Basil Bunting: Briggflatts* (Northumberland: Bloodaxe, 2009).

CRITICAL AND BIOGRAPHICAL STUDIES INCLUDING CHAPTERS ON BUNTING

Alexander, Michael and McGonigal, James (eds.), *Sons of Ezra: British Poets and Ezra Pound* (Amsterdam: Rodopi, 1995). An important study which contains chapters by Roy Fisher, Donald Davie and Charles Tomlinson. James McGonigal's 'An XYZ of Reading: Basil Bunting in the British Tradition' is instructive as it also considers pre-modernist sources.

Alldritt, Keith, *The Poet as Spy: The Life and Wild Times of Basil Bunting* (London: Arum Press, 1998). This is, in effect, the first full-length biographical study of Bunting. The title sets the tone and Alldritt covers a great deal of useful ground, especially regarding the war years and the poet's involvement in intelligence work.

Basil Bunting: Briggflatts (Northumberland: Bloodaxe, 2009) Includes CD of *Briggflatts* read by Basil Bunting and DVD of Peter Bell's film of Basil Bunting. As well as the text of *Briggflatts* and accompanying notes, the publication comes with 'A Note on *Briggflatts*' (1989) and 'The Poet's Point of View' (1966), which is often known as 'A Statement'. Here Bunting promotes his sonic principles of poetry.

Burnett, David, *Basil Bunting* (Durham: Durham University Library, 1987), a 12-page pamphlet.

Caddel, Richard (ed.), *Sharp Study and Long Toil: Basil Bunting Special Issue* (Durham: A Durham University Journal in association with the Basil Bunting Poetry Centre, 1995). A useful collection of essays, reviews, poems dedicated to the memory of Eric Mottram.

—— and Flowers, Anthony (eds.), *Basil Bunting: A Northern Life* (Durham: Newcastle Libraries and Information Service in association with the Basil Bunting Poetry Centre, 1997). Richard Caddel, who writes the introduction to *Complete Poems*, was a distinguished Bunting scholar and a poet in his own right. *A Northern Life* positions Bunting in his Northumbrian milieu. The book comes with some interesting photographs, including pictures of Bunting with Allen Ginsberg.

Corcoran, Neil, *English Poetry Since 1940* (London and New York: Longman, 1993). The third chapter – 'A Modernism of Place' – provides a useful account of the poetry of David Jones and Basil Bunting.

Davie, Donald, *The Poet in the Imaginary Museum: Essays of Two Decades* ed. Barry Alpert (Manchester: Carcanet, 1977). A variegated collection of essays which deals with, *inter alia,* the Movement, Pound, Eliot, Yeats, as well as an important essay 'English and American in *Briggflatts*' in which Davie claims that Bunting's achievement 'is what English poets must assimilate and go on from.'

———, *Under Briggflatts: A History of Poetry in Great Britain 1960–1988* (Manchester: Carcanet, 1989). A fairly wide-ranging compendium of essays and observations which pivots notionally on the publication of *Briggflatts* in 1966. The title itself implies the centrality of Bunting's poem in the period under investigation.

Day, Gary, and Docherty, Brian (eds.), *British Poetry from the 1950s to the 1990s: Politics and Art* (London: Macmillan, 1997). Dennis Brown's chapter on *Briggflatts* makes for a useful contribution as he considers how Bunting, like David Jones, 'has created a historically allusive and linguistically canny long poem in the era of the short, idiosyncratically [. . .] voiced lyric.'

Forde, Victoria, *The Poetry of Basil Bunting* (Newcastle upon Tyne: Bloodaxe, 1991). This was, in many ways, a pioneering study in which Sister Forde, who knew Bunting over many years, draws on letters and correspondence to provide an important critical study of the poet's life and work.

Guedalla, Roger, *Basil Bunting: A Bibliography of Works and Criticism* (Norwood, PA: Norwood Editions, 1973).

Hamburger, Michael, The *Truth of Poetry: Tensions in Modern Poetry from Baudelaire to the 1960s* (London: Weidenfeld and Nicolson, 1969). An ambitious, wide-ranging study, almost 'an encyclopaedia of modern poetry', with insightful references to Bunting.

Lesch, Barbara E., 'Basil Bunting: A Major British Modernist', PhD Dissertation (University of Wisconsin, 1979). A highly informative early account of Bunting's work which Victoria Forde refers to in her study of Bunting.

McGonigal, James and Price, Richard (eds.), *The Star You Steer By: Basil Bunting and British Modernism* (Amsterdam: Rodopi, 2000). An excellent compendium of essays which came out to complement the publication of *Complete Poems* in 2000. Among the contributors we find Roy Fisher, Richard Caddel, Philip Hobsbaum, Victoria Forde, as well as useful pieces by the editors themselves.

Makin, Peter, *Bunting: The Shaping of His Verse* (Oxford: Clarendon Press, 1992). This must count as one of the most important studies of Bunting's verse. Makin combines close readings, cultural context and an intricately researched historical hinterland. Excellent chapters on early English saints and warriors as well as a careful examination of the the Lindisfarne Gospels and their importance to Bunting in the composition of *Briggflatts*.

——— (ed.), *Basil Bunting on Poetry* (Baltimore: Johns Hopkins University Press, 1999). Makin tells us that 'These lectures are the fruit of a poet's brief career in late life as a university lecturer.' In effect, Bunting returns to the significance of rhythm and reveals his interest in Wyatt, Spenser, Wordsworth, Whitman, Pound and Zukofsky. There's also a useful chapter on the Lindisfarne Gospels or *The Codex* with helpful illustrations.

Quartermain, Peter, *Basil Bunting: Poet of the North* (Durham: Basil Bunting Poetry centre, 1990). An 18-page pamphlet which considers the ideological implications of Bunting's Northumbrian provenance.

Terrell, Carroll F. (ed.), *Basil Bunting: Man and Poet* (Orono, Maine: National Poetry Foundation, 1981). This is an early, all-important American publication that considers both biographical and critical perspectives. Contributors include Hugh Kenner, Eric Mottram, Victoria Forde, Donald Davie and Anthony Suter.

Tuma, Keith, *Fishing By Obstinate Isles: Modern and Postmodern British Poetry and American Readers* (Evanston, Ill.: Northwestern University Press, 1998). Tuma takes his title from Pound's *Hugh Selwyn Mauberley* and the reference is useful in that Pound's vitriolic valediction to England prefigures later, jaundiced American views regarding post-1945 British poetry. Tuma is keen to re-consider the lost modernist poetics within British traditions and not only does he write interestingly about 'Anglo-American' relations in poetry but he also dedicates chapters to the British poet Mina Loy and Bunting's *Briggflatts*.

Williams, Jonathan (ed.), *Madeira & Toasts for Basil Bunting's 75th Birthday* (Dentdale: Jargon Society, 1975). A buoyant festschrift that includes poems, anecdotes, sketches and critical appraisals with a rich array of contributors including Hugh Kenner, Roy Fisher, Edwin Morgan, Charles Tomlinson, Tom Raworth, Hugh MacDiarmid.

SELECTED ARTICLES AND SPECIAL JOURNAL ISSUES

Agenda, 16/1 (Spring 1978): Basil Bunting Special Issue.
Bête Noire, 2/3 (Spring 1987): Basil Bunting Special Issue.
Clucas, Garth, 'Basil Bunting: A Chronology', *Poetry Information*, 19 (Autumn 1978).
Connolly, Cyril, 'Out of Northumbria', *Sunday Times* (12 Feb. 1967), 53.
Cox, Kenneth, 'The Aesthetic of Basil Bunting', *Agenda*, 4/3 (Autumn 1966), 20–8.
———, 'A Commentary on Basil Bunting's *Villon*', *Agenda*, 16/1 (Spring 1978), 20–36.
———, 'Basil Bunting', *Scripsi*, 3/2–3 (August 1985), 1–5.
Creeley, Robert, 'A Note on Basil Bunting', *Agenda*, 4/3 (Autumn 1966),

18–19.

'Exotic Northumbria', *Times Literary Supplement*, 16 February 1967.

Georgia Straight Writing Supplement, 6 (18–24 November 1970): Basil Bunting Special Issue.

Gunn, Thom, 'What the Slowworm Said', *PN Review* 27, 7/1 (1982), 26–9.

Hall, Anthea, 'Basil Bunting Explains how a Poet Works', *Journal* (17 July 1965), 7.

Kleinzahler, August, 'Remembering Bunting', *Scripsi*, 3/2–3 (August 1985).

MacKay, Brent, 'Bunting as Teacher', *Conjunctions*, 8 (1985), 181.

Paideuma 9/1 (Spring 1980): Basil Bunting Special Issue.

Pickard, Tom, 'Serving My Time to a Trade', *Paideuma*, 9/1 (Spring 1980), 155–63.

Poetry Information 19 (Autumn 1978): Basil Bunting Special Issue.

Quartermain, Peter, and Tallman, Warren, 'Basil Bunting Talks about *Briggflatts*', *Georgia Straight Writing Supplement*, 6 (1970), n.p.

Read, Herbert, 'Basil Bunting: Music or Meaning', *Agenda*, 4/3 (Autumn 1966), 4–10.

Scripsi, 1/3–4 (April 1982): Basil Bunting Special Issue.

Suter, Anthony, 'Musical Structure in the Poetry of Basil Bunting', *Agenda*, 16/1 (1978), 46–54.

———, 'Time and the Literary Past in the Poetry of Basil Bunting', *Contemporary Literature*, 12/4 (Autumn 1971), 510–26.

———, 'The Writer in the Mirror. Basil Bunting and T. S. Eliot: Parody and Parallel', *Paideuma*, 9/1 (Spring 1980), 89–99.

Swann, Brian, 'Basil Bunting of Northumberland', *St. Andrews Review*, 4/2 (Spring–Summer 1977), 33–41.

Tomlinson, Charles, 'Experience into Music: The Poetry of Basil Bunting', *Agenda*, 4/3 (Autumn 1966), 11–17.

Wickens, G. M., 'The Persian Conception of Artistic Unity in Poetry and its Implications in Other Fields', *Bulletin of the School of Oriental and African Studies*, XIV (1952), 704–5.

Woof, R. S., 'Basil Bunting's Poetry', *Stand*, 8/2 (1966), 28–34.

Zukofsky, Louis, Letters to, 1930–64. Harry Ransom Humanities Research Center, University of Texas at Austin. Includes many letters from Basil Bunting.

INTERVIEWS

Craven, Peter and Heyward, Michael, 'An Interview with Basil Bunting', *Scripsi*, 1/3–4 (April 1982), 27–31.

Figgis, Sean and McAllister, Andrew, 'Basil Bunting: The Last Interview', *Bête Noire*, 2/3 (Spring 1987), 22–51.

Paul Johnstone, '[Two Interviews]', *Meantime*, 1 (April 1977), 67–80.

Mottram, Eric, 'Conversation with Basil Bunting on the Occasion of his 75th Birthday, *Poetry Information* 19 (Autumn 1978), 3–10.

Reagan, Dale, 'An Interview with Basil Bunting', *Montemora*, 3 (Spring 1977), 67–80.

Williams, Jonathan and Meyer, Tom, 'A Conversation with Basil Bunting', *Poetry Information* 19 (1978), 37–47.

Williams, Jonathan (ed.), *Descant on Rawthey's Madrigal: Conversations with Basil Bunting* (Lexington, Ky.: Gnomon Press, 1968). An invaluable interview with Bunting which serves as a biographical sketch as well as providing insights into the poet's working practice.

ANTHOLOGIES

Alvarez, A. (ed.), *The New Poetry* (London: Penguin, 1962).

Allnutt, Gillian, D'Aguiar, Fred, Edwards, Ken and Mottram, Eric (eds.), *The New British Poetry 1968–88* (London: Paladin Grafton Books, 1988).

Conquest, Robert (ed.), *New Lines* (London: Macmillan, 1956).

Byrne, James and Pollard, Clare (eds.), *Voice Recognition: 21 Poets for the 21st Century* (Northumberland: Bloodaxe, 2009).

Enright, D. J. (ed.), *Poets of the 1950s* (Tokyo: The Keneyusha Press, 1955).

Caddel, Richard and Quartermain, Peter (eds.), *Other: British and Irish Poetry Since 1970* (Hanover, NH, and London: Wesleyan University Press, 1999).

Hulse, Michael, Kennedy, David and Morley, David (eds.), *The New Poetry* (Northumberland: Bloodaxe, 1993).

Keene, Donald, (ed.), *Anthology of Japanese Literature from the Earliest Era to the Mid-Nineteenth Century* (New York: UNESCO, 1955).

Lumsden, Roddy and Stonborough, Eloise (eds.), *The Salt Book of Younger Poets* (London: Salt Publishing 2011).

Morrison, Blake and Motion, Andrew (eds.), *The Penguin Book of Contemporary British Verse* (London: Penguin, 1982).

Sinclair, Ian (ed.), *Conductors of Chaos: A Poetry Anthology* (London: Picador, 1996).

Tuma, Keith, *Anthology of Twentieth-Century British and Irish Poetry* (New York: Oxford University Press, 2001).

GENERAL BIBLIOGRAPHY INCLUDING CITED TEXTS

Bacigalupo, Massimo, 'Scrittori Anglofoni in Liguria nel Novecento', *Bilancio della Leteteratura del Novocento in Liguria* ed. Giovanni Ponte (Genoa: Academia Ligure di Scienze e Lettere, 2002).

———— (ed.), *Ezra Pound: Un Poeta a* Rapallo (Genoa, 1985).

———— and Pratt, William (eds.), *Tigullio Itineraries: Ezra Pound and Friends*, from 'Ezra Pound, Language and Persona' (Ezra Pound International Conference) *Quaderni de Palazzo Serra 15* (Rapallo: Università degli Studi di Genova, 2005).

Barry, Peter, *Poetry Wars: British Poetry of the 1970s and the Battle of Earls Court* (Cambridge: Salt Publishing, 2006).

Basho, Matsuo, *Basho's Journey: The Literary Prose of Matsuo Basho* trans. David Landis Barnhill (Albany, NY: Suny Press, 2005).

Bate, Jonathan, *The Song of the Earth* (London: Picador, 2000). A series of ecological readings of English literature which speaks of *Briggflatts* as 'a deeply Wordsworthian autobiographical meditation on loss and recovery in which identity is forged in place.'

Beasley, Rebecca, *Theorists of Modernist Poetry: T. S. Eliot, T. E. Hulme, Ezra Pound* (London and New York: Routledge, 2007).

Bloom, Harold, *The Anxiety of Influence: A Theory of Poetry* (London: Oxford University Press, 1975).

Brown, Gordon, (ed.), *High on the Walls: An Anthology Celebrating Twenty-Five Years of Poetry Readings at Morden Tower* (Newcastle upon Tyne: Morden Tower/Bloodaxe, 1990) a homage to the iconic tower from a rich array of poets who have read there.

Burton, Richard, *A Strong Song Tows Us: The Life of Basil Bunting* (Oxford: Infinite Ideas, 2013).

Clark, Timothy, *Charles Tomlinson* (Tavistock: Northcote House Publishers: Writers and their Work, 1999).

Dante, *Inferno*, trans. Robin Kirkpatrick (London; Penguin Classics, 2006).

Davie, Donald, *Ezra Pound: Poet as Sculptor* (New York: Oxford University Press, 1964).

————, *Thomas Hardy and British Poetry* (London: Routledge and Kegan Paul, 1973).

————, *Older Masters: Essays and Reflections on English and American Literature* (Manchester: Carcanet, 1992).

————, *Collected Poems* (Manchester: Carcanet, 2002).

————, *Purity of Diction in English Verse* and *Articulate Energy* (Manchester: Carcanet, 2006).

Eliot, T. S., *Selected Prose of* (London: Faber and Faber, 1975).

————, *The Sacred Wood: Essays on Poetry and Criticism* (London: Faber and Faber, 1997).

Forbes, Peter, 'Talking about the New Generation', *Poetry Review*, 84/1 (Spring 1994), 4–6.

Jones, Peter, *Imagist Poetry* (London: Penguin Books, 1985).

Kenner, Hugh, *A Sinking Island: The Modern English Writers* (London: Barrie and Jenkins, 1988). The book is dedicated to Basil Bunting.

Larkin, Philip, *All What Jazz: a Record Diary 1961–71* (London: Faber and Faber, 1970).

———, *Required Writing: Miscellaneous Pieces 1955–1982* (London: Faber and Faber, 1983).

———, *Collected Poems* (London: Faber and Faber, 1988).

Leverson, Michael (ed.), *The Cambridge Companion to Modernism* (Cambridge: Cambridge University Press, 1999).

Il Mare: Supplemento Letterario ed. Società Letteraria Rapallo (Rapallo: Commune di Rapallo, 1999).

Morrison, Blake, *The Movement: English Poetry and Fiction of the 1950s* (Oxford: Oxford University Press, 1980).

O'Brien, Sean, 'As Deep as England', *Poetry Review* , 102/1 (Spring 2012), 54–69.

Perloff, Marjorie, 'The Two Poetries: An Introduction', *Contemporary Literature*, 18 (Summer 1977), 263–78.

Pickard, Tom, *High on the Walls*. Preface by Basil Bunting (London: Fulcrum Press, 1967).

Pound, Ezra, *The Cantos* (London: Faber and Faber, 1987).

———, *ABC of Reading* (London: Faber and Faber, 1991).

Pound, Omar, *Arabic and Persian Poems in English*. Foreword by Basil Bunting (New York: New Directions, 1970).

Rabaté, Jean-Michel, *1913: The Cradle of Modernism* (Oxford: Blackwell Publishing, 2007).

Robinson, Peter, *Twentieth Century Poetry: Selves and Situations* (Oxford: Oxford University Press, 2003). See the chapter 'Basil Bunting's Emigrant Ballads', 39–48.

———, *Poetry and Translation: The Art of the Impossible* (Liverpool: Liverpool University Press, 2010).

Schmidt, Michael, *Reading Modern Poetry* (London: Routledge, 1989).

Share, Don (ed.), *Bunting's Persia: Translations by Basil Bunting* (Chicago: Flood Editions, 2012).

Stannard, Julian, *The Poetic Achievements of Donald Davie and Charles Tomlinson: Explanding Vision, Voice and Rhythm in Late Twentieth-Century English Poetry* (Lewiston, NY: Edwin Mellen Press, 2010).

Tomlinson, Charles, *New Collected Poems* (Manchester: Carcanet/Oxford Poets, 2009).

——— (ed.), *William Carlos Williams: Selected Poems* (Harmondsworth: Penguin, 1976).

Tytell, John, *Ezra Pound: The Solitary Volcano* (London: Bloomsbury, 1987).

Villon, François, *Complete Works of*, trans. Anthony Bonner with an introduction by William Carlos Williams (New York: Bantam Books, 1960).

———, *Selected Poems*, trans. Peter Dale (London: Penguin, 1988).

Williams, William Carlos, *The Autobiography of William Carlos Williams* (New York; Random House, 1951).

Zukofsky, Louis, *A Test of Poetry* (Middletown, Conn.: Wesleyan University Press, 2000).

Index